CHRONICLES
—— OF THE ——
BRITISH OCCUPATION
OF
LONG ISLAND

CHRONICLES

─── OF THE ───

BRITISH OCCUPATION

OF

LONG ISLAND

DAVID M. GRIFFIN

THE
History
PRESS

Published by The History Press
Charleston, SC
www.historypress.com

Front cover, bottom: *Advance of the Enemy*, Alfred Wordsworth Thompson painting, before 1896. *Public domain.*

Back cover, top: *Brooklyn, Long Island (View of the Village Green)*, circa 1778. *Metropolitan Museum of Art.*

First published 2023

Manufactured in the United States

ISBN 9781467151399

Library of Congress Control Number: 2023932161

Notice: The information in this book is true and complete to the best of our knowledge. It is offered without guarantee on the part of the author or The History Press. The author and The History Press disclaim all liability in connection with the use of this book.

To the memory of Henry Onderdonk Jr.

CONTENTS

ACKNOWLEDGEMENTS

In researching and writing these chronicles, I have many people and associations to thank.

My continued thanks go out to all the historical societies of Long Island and local history libraries, many of which helped me in my research of this work.

A special thank-you goes out to Georgette Case, Riverhead town historian; Susan Kovarik of the Historical Society of the Westburys; Joan Mcgee, historian of the Village of Lloyd Harbor; Karen Martin of the Huntington Historical Society; Andrea Meyer of the Long Island Collection at the East Hampton Library; Ross Schwalm of the Johannes Schwalm Historical Association; and Edna Davis Giffen of the Miller Place Mt. Sinai Historical Society.

Much appreciated are the historical documents and maps and the help of the staff at the William L. Clements Library at the University of Michigan in Ann Arbor, Michigan.

A special thank-you is owed to Leah Grandy of the University of New Brunswick Archives and Special Collections/Loyalist Collection. Her in-depth help and research assistance is much appreciated.

Thank you to the continued assistance of the staff at the Long Island Studies Institute at Hofstra University.

Many thanks to Richard Gachot and Ted Gachot of the Gachot family formerly of Westbury, New York, and to their father, Richard Gachot, who was a great recorder of local history.

I am also grateful for the continual assistance of Zachary Studenroth, town historian of the Town of Southampton and Long Island architectural historian.

Thanks to Gary Haglich of the Nassau County Department of Parks and Recreation for continuing to support me in my research of Old Jericho.

Thank you to Brad and Robert Bocksel of Aquebogue for their insight and inspiration.

Much appreciated is my friendship with Don Troiani. His continuous aid and knowledge in period artifact identification has helped me greatly.

Thank you to researcher and author Don Hagist for his inspiration and continuous help with my own research and writing.

Thank you to the Suffolk County Historical Society Archives for their help and support in my research.

Also appreciated are my friends who helped me research historical preservation and supported and inspired me. Thank you, William Salas of the Smithtown Public Library, for your support and inspiration, Claire Bellerjeau for your friendship and inspiration through your continued work on *Remember Liss* and Steve Boerner of the Cedar Swamp Historical Society for your friendship and continued efforts to keep local and Long Island history alive.

Thank you to my mother and father, my family and especially my brother Dan for his support, continued enthusiasm and work for the United Empire Loyalist Association of Canada.

Thank you to The History Press for allowing this book to be created. Special thanks to Banks Smither of The History Press for his support and guidance.

INTRODUCTION

I continue to be fortunate in being able to further my personal research of the eighteenth century in the New York City area. My research, primarily focused on the years of the Revolutionary War in New York City and Long Island, has allowed me to come closer to understanding the day-to-day experiences of the people living during this period. Before a time of photography and modern technology, the eighteenth century remains a hidden world. Its culture and environments are foreign to our own. My own personal studies involving researching and writing about the landscape and people of the time give me personal glimpses into what it was like to live within this hidden world.

In the process of this exploration, I have come across interesting stories and intriguing insights from the period. Some have been expanded on in my independent articles and personal writings. In my own acquiring of period memoirs and personal stories, and my private collecting of period artifacts, I have added greatly to my understanding of the time. This present title, *Chronicles of the British Occupation of Long Island*, endeavors to articulate on this collection of work and research. It is set during the years of the British Occupation of Long Island between 1776 and 1783.

Historically, it is well recorded that by the fall of 1776, the New York region had been conquered by the British forces after the Battle of Long Island and had become an occupied region for the remaining years of the Revolutionary War. The British occupation of New York City and the Long

Island area was the longest continuous occupation of any area on the East Coast of the entire war. Long Island was divided in its beliefs regarding the proposed separation from England. The western half of Long Island had significant numbers of Loyalists, and the eastern half of the island swayed more toward Patriotism and independence.

After the occupation, the island became an important supply resource for the British army in New York City and a defensive front line for the American forces in New England. Foraging supplies was the primary focus of active British and Loyalist troops on Long Island. The supplies were collected in magazines and then moved to the island's shores and harbors; then they were moved by water to New York City to supply the large troop populations within the city. Fortifications were established along the shores to protect the supply. The American army carried out a number of offensive actions before the Battle of Long Island and throughout the years of occupation from the Connecticut shores of the Long Island Sound. All were efforts to disrupt British supply lines. Loyalist sympathizers and American Patriots were caught in the middle of this struggle. Many local citizens who supported independence were forced to take refuge in Connecticut due to their support for American liberty. Those supporters who chose to remain suffered greatly. Many were singled out by the British occupying forces for use of their resources and property as a form of punishment. Some who remained were forced to sign an oath of allegiance to King George III for their own security. Former neighbors were pitted against each other, and some Loyalists on the island were attacked by their former townsmen. It was not at all strange to find families divided along political lines. This seven-year struggle on Long Island must always be thought of first and foremost as a civil war and a time of great suffering for all inhabitants on the island, regardless of which side they were on.

General William Howe, the conquering commander of the region, in a proclamation on August 23, 1776, offered pardon and protection to the loyal inhabitants of Long Island, who had been "forced into rebellion," and he gave encouragement to "those who chose to take up arms for the restoration of order and good government within the island."[1] Brigadier General William Erskine's proclamation on August 29, 1776, called upon the inhabitants of Suffolk County to lay down their arms and provide the troops with cattle, wagons and horses. If they failed to show "a dutiful submission to all respects," Erskine warned, he would march his troops "without delay into the country" and "lay waste the property of the disobedient, as persons unworthy of His Majesty's clemency."[2] This British commander's comments

The Relief (1781), by Henry William Bunbury. *From the Anne S.K. Brown Military Collection, Brown Digital Repository, Brown University Library.*

give us a glimpse into the personal differences in strategy for the management of the occupied region. These differences give us some foresight into the events that were to follow on Long Island.

Probably the best primary histories that recorded the historical events that occurred during the years of the British occupation—and which aided in my research—are the works of Henry Onderdonk Jr., including his two books, *Documents and Letters Intended to Illustrate the Revolutionary Incidents of Queens County, etc.* and *Revolutionary Incidents of Suffolk and Kings Counties, etc.* Both of these works were written in the nineteenth century but relied heavily on firsthand personal interviews with eighteenth-century participants and survivors from the Revolutionary War. They prove to be historically accurate based on cross-references with other Revolutionary War–period documents. Another important work of note is *The Refugees of 1776 from Long Island to Connecticut* by Frederic Mather.

Some orderly books of Loyalist regiments recorded the day-to-day troop activity on Long Island. Two of these sources are *Orderly Book of the Maryland Loyalists Regiment, June 18th, 1778, to October 12th, 1778* and *Orderly Book of the Three Battalions of Loyalist Commanded by Brigadier-General Oliver De Lancey 1776–*

1778. Also, the Archives of Canada provides valuable information in the form of period muster roles and Loyalist records.

Other than the previously noted sources, *The Papers of George Washington, Revolutionary War Series*, gives accounts of events and troop locations behind the British lines that were recorded within Washington's intelligence network. Well known are the many volumes of research regarding espionage on both sides of the war. This topic is well documented by many authors and is not covered within this book unless a particular spy record references pertinent troop locations helpful to the narrative.

Lastly, a most valuable resource can be found in land records and land transfers and ownership. These can aid in locating historical spots that have since been lost on Long Island. I sometimes find that period land records are lacking information on transfers; in some cases, these were unrecorded confiscations by the British army that occurred during the war. Many local Patriots fled Long Island for Connecticut, leaving their homes abandoned and/or in another person's care. This also occurs in records of particular historical individuals, who just seem to disappear. After digging deeper, many of these individuals are found out to be outcasts or survivors who took refuge and acted on their own beliefs of loyalty to one side or the other. I sometimes like to refer to this as the "dark ages" of Long Island's history.

It is within this dark age of the island's history that this book hopes to illuminate the participants and places of this truly trying period. What I find most lacking in the recorded histories are insights into the personal experiences of the people who lived through these years of occupation. People from both sides of the struggle experienced hard times on Long Island. In my research, I have wanted to understand more about how both the conquering army and the local civilians experienced the occupation. Where did they live and how? How did they suffer? What were the ideas, attitudes and worries of the differing parties? What were their beliefs, and how did they differ between the many political and religious parties who lived on the island during the war?

There exists one piece of writing from 1859 called *Personal Recollections of the American Revolution, A Private Journal. Prepared from Authentic Domestic Records*, written by Lydia Minturn Post, that touches on an individual person's experiences. The work, which initially comes across as being an authentic diary from the eighteenth century, is in fact a fictionalized diary of a woman who lived during the Revolutionary War on Long Island. Although it is not a true historical account, the work has great merit, as it brings to light the many challenges experienced by the people who were

A Long Island Homestead (1889), by Charles Henry Miller and Barry August. *From the Charles Henry Miller Digital Collection, Special Collections and University Archives, Stony Brook University Libraries.*

Henry Post House, Old Westbury (photograph taken before 1870). *Courtesy of the Historical Society of the Westburys.*

living at the time. A twentieth-century article written by Sarah Buck that analyzes the book by Post concludes:

> *The story of Mary, the fictitious alter ego of Lydia Minturn Post, can be interpreted simultaneously as a recreation of revolutionary Long Island; a contribution to American Patriotic folklore; and a sentimental antebellum novel. The reader learns of a brave Patriot soldier, a caring Tory Anglican minister, a wounded British soldier, and a harassed Quaker family. These characters interact in a divided Long Island community, severely affected by the harsh British occupation.*[3]

While conducting research about the book and its author, Lydia Post, it was interesting to discover that the writing is a dramatization of common experiences and that a character in the book named Henry Pattison is in fact derived from a true historical person named Henry Post, who just happens to be the author's grandfather. Historically, Henry Post was a Quaker who lived during the American Revolution in the Westbury area of Long Island with his wife, Mary Titus, and their six sons. Within his house were quartered

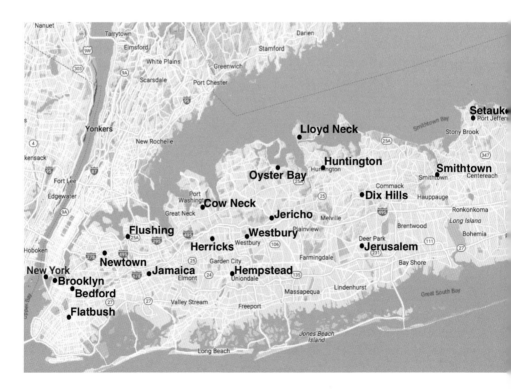

British forces. The house still exists, and supposedly, Major Crief died within the house. Hessian soldiers also cut down trees on the property and piled them along the roadway, where they were carted away to build forts and barracks away from Westbury.[4]

In 1960, Richard and Irene Gachot purchased and renovated this same circa 1761 Post house. They found hand-hewn beams and period mantelpieces in the house, along with eighteenth-century ammunition and artifacts embedded in the walls.[5] The house retains much of its early colonial Long Island farmhouse character.

While reading the Post diary, I found references to specific places on Long Island that are elsewhere recorded in period sources and, in fact, true to Revolutionary War records. Many events or details within the diary are too close to actual historical accounts to be made up. In my mind, it is certain that the writer of the Post diary used some form of authentic diary record to construct the narrative. In light of this research, I would like to consider the Post diary a valuable resource for understanding the social history of the region. I will make reference to particular parts of this diary within this book when they aid in enlightening or validating other recorded histories.

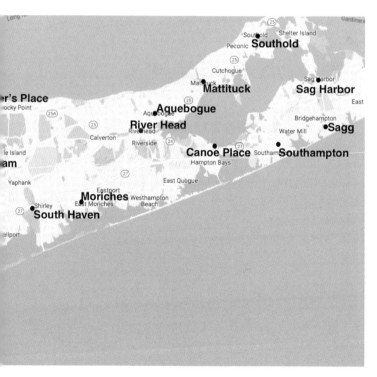

Map of the primary towns and villages on Long Island during the period of the British Occupation, 1776–1783. *Map by the author.*

Long Island in 1776 had become one of the most populated areas of the state of New York. Long Island's population at the time of the war was around 28,000. New York City's population at that time was just under 22,000.[6] The island's length was substantial at 130 miles, and its land mass was filled with many towns and villages. A report in the papers of George Washington from January 1779 has the British forces estimated at around 3,800 to 4,000 men quartered on Long Island.[7] These numbers changed from year to year, so at certain times, the numbers could have been smaller or even doubled from this. The size of these forces and Long Island's civilian population implies that there were many encounters and experiences taking place between the two groups during the years of occupation.

The chapters to follow are a dialogue about the events that transpired during the years of the British occupation of Long Island. It is not a chronological history but a mixing of stories and accounts, along with historical analysis by the author. Not all of the stories are historically accurate. Even so, these records articulate a general experience of the population at the time. Many historical encounters have taken on their own exaggerations in later writings and memory. Many of the names of characters have been passed down incorrectly. Where I am able, historical characters and events have been researched via primary sources to try to authenticate their true stories and names. Many new sources, which may not have been available to authors of the past, are available to researchers today.

The following chapters are titled as themes relevant to the time of the British occupation. These titles would have been common vocabulary to the local population. My former book, *Lost British Forts of Long Island*, tells the history of the British defenses established across Long Island and of the struggles for their control. This work should also be considered a sister book to this title.

The map below shows the network of primary towns and villages on Long Island during the period in which the stories of this book unfold. Although the map does not represent all of the period towns and locations of the time, it does set up a general backdrop, showing most of the locations in which the stories to follow take place.

Note: Transcribed quotations appear in the book in their original form as documented from their sources. Any errors in spelling and grammar are characteristic of the language of the period and are transcribed exactly as they were recorded.

1

QUARTERING

The housing of troops in New York City and on Long Island during the Revolutionary War was a massive endeavor. Thousands of forces were quartered and encamped in the region, and a continuous and changing need for shelter was required for all the occupied forces for the duration of the war.

The main sources of housing in New York City and Queens and Suffolk Counties were the existing building stocks in the region. Taverns, inns, meetinghouses and private houses were confiscated in part or in whole for housing needs. Where there were not enough existing buildings, the occupiers built rustic huts or barracks. In the milder weather, these troops utilized reusable tents.[8]

In 1765, the English Parliament issued a law requiring colonists to provide accommodations, supplies and transportation to British soldiers by enacting the Quartering Act. The Quartering Act, however, prohibited British soldiers from entering private houses.[9] In the peacetime years following the French and Indian War, the law was abided by within the colonies. In a time of war, such as during the Revolutionary War, this quartering (also known as billeting) became a necessity for the British army, and the restrictions of the Quartering Act no longer applied. Billeting was so called from the billet, or ticket, that soldiers showed to the masters of private houses as their warrant to occupy a part of it.[10]

By the mid- to late eighteenth century, the use of colonists' houses had progressed. Larger homes, often those with two stories and six or more rooms, had become spaces that allowed for some separation between the family and non-family members. This separation allowed family members to experience a deepened sense of privacy within their homes. Billeting in a time of war again challenged these new aspiring notions of privacy in the home. Americans soon saw the act of billeting British soldiers as a symbol of British oppression in the colonies.[11]

In 1776, before the British conquered New York City, those with Tory affiliations on Long Island were at risk of having their property confiscated and their homes occupied by rebel troops. Dr. Samuel Martin, who owned Rock Hall in present-day Lawrence, New York, had his home ransacked by rebel troops for arms and ammunition in 1776, and his house was occupied for a time by these soldiers. He was also imprisoned and kept under guard for some time.[12]

After Long Island was occupied by the British, the act of billeting troops became necessary, due to the size of the forces needed to reside in the area. In this changing dynamic, the Whigs, who had supported independence and remained on the island, were at great risk of their property being taken and their homes and resources being confiscated for use by the British. Henry Onderdonk Jr. illustrates the act of billeting British soldiers on Long Island at the time.

> During the summer British troops were off island on active service, or if a few remained here they abode under tents; but in winter they were hutted on the sunny side of a hill, or else distributed in farmer's houses. A British officer accompanied by a justice of the piece or some prominent loyalist as a guide, rode around the country, and from actual inspection decided how many soldiers each house could receive, and this number was chalked on the door. The only notification was, "Madam we have come to take a billet on your house." If a house had but one fireplace it was passed by, as the soldiers were not intended to form part of the family. A double house for the officers or single house with a kitchen for the privates was just the thing. The soldiers were quartered in the kitchen, and the inner door nailed up so the soldiers could not intrude on the household. They, however, often became intimate with the family and sometime intermarried.[13]

Onderdonk's writings give further specifics:

> Each Family was allowed one fire-place, and the officers fixed the number of soldiers to be billeted in each house, which was usually from 10 to 20.

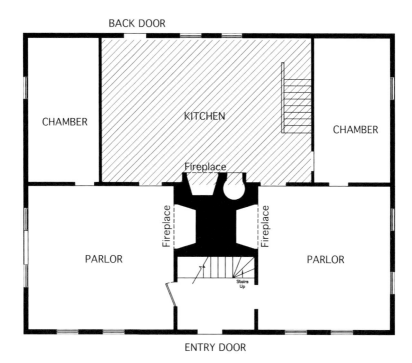

A plan layout of a typical colonial house on Long Island showing the centrality of the kitchen space at the top center of the drawing. *Drawing by the author.*

A photograph of a period kitchen preserved and displayed at the William Miller House, Miller Place. *Photograph by author.*

They had three tiers of hammocks, one above the other, ranged round the room, and made of boards stripped from some fence or outbuilding [14]

The kitchen was not the only space used for quartering; other rooms also sufficed. In an order from Mr. Cutler Forage Master, he directs Mr. Schenck of Cow Neck, "Finding that your house will justly admit to receiving a Billet, you are therefore Directed to Provide Mr. Cutler. Forrage Master to the Hessian Chassure Corps, with one good Room. The use of the Kitchen and place for his servant To sleep in." [15]

The kitchen space was essentially the heart, or center, of the eighteenth-century home. It was a much more rustic and functional space than the rest of the house. This, along with the fact that kitchens normally had a fireplace and back entry door to the house, may have contributed greatly to its choice for use as troop accommodations.

The kitchen in all of the farmhouses of all the colonies was the most cheerful, homelike, and picturesque room in the house; indeed, it was in town houses as well. The walls were often bare, the rafters dingy; windows were small, the furniture meagre; but the kitchen had a warm, glowing heart that spread light and welcome, and made the poor room a home. [16]

One can imagine that this choice for quartering in the house was frustrating for the inhabitants, as they then had limited access or no access at all to the kitchen space. Other spaces and formal parlors would have had to suffice for daily use and sometimes cooking. The scale of these homes was also small. A family would need to endure the sharing of important common resources within close quarters. Today, one only needs to tour a preserved colonial house on Long Island to imagine the cramped reality of life in the eighteenth century. The kitchen was also the most comfortable room in the house in wintertime, with its continuous use of the hearth for cooking. The bedrooms of the typical colonial house were seldom warmed. [17]

Within the Lydia Post diary, her observances seem to concur with the quartering of troops in her own house and their selection of the kitchen as their place of habitation. Her writing demonstrates the fears and anxieties of having soldiers in her house. Her writing exhibits a prejudice toward the German soldiers, which may have been typical of the time. Most likely, whether the intruders were British or German, all those who had to endure billeting shared similar feelings.

Once a month the Hessians go to headquarters for their rations, including spirits, and then for three days they are for the most part given up to intoxication, and we have trying and grievous scenes to go through; fighting, brawls, drumming, and fifing and dancing the night long; card and dice playing, and every abomination going on under our very roofs! The noise from the kitchen, which they always occupy, is terrifying. The door opening into the rest of the house is nailed fast, but the inmates are continually in dread of having their dwellings burnt over their heads.[18]

She also records:

This neighborhood is still infested with the odious Hessians. They are so filthy and lazy, lounging about all day long, smoking and sleeping. The patience of the good Friends is inexhaustible. After filling up their parlors, kitchens, and bed-rooms, the whole winter with chests, liquor-casks, hammocks, bird-cages, guns, boots and powder-flasks, they were last week ordered to Jamaica. Oh the rejoicing![19]

As mentioned previously, the Lydia Post diary makes reference to Henry Pattison, a character based on an actual Long Island resident named Henry Post. The Revolutionary War–period Post House, which is still standing today, was purchased by Richard and Irene Gachot in the 1960s. Richard Gachot, who was also a local historian, found eighteenth-century artifacts in the house during a renovation.

Richard's son Ted Gachot recollects, "As collectors, the Gachots were drawn to the beauty of simple means but also to character—the sense of a story behind a piece. They eventually discovered that the musket balls in their home were from Hessian soldiers, garrisoned there during the Revolution, shooting stuffed parrots they'd nailed to the walls."[20]

A correspondence between this author and Ted Gachot, in preparing this book, helped uncover the story about the findings. He mentioned that his father, Richard Gachot, learned a great deal about early Westbury history from discussions with then aged local Quaker neighbors. He seemed to remember hearing from his father that these neighbors told the story of Hessian mercenaries who quartered in the Post house during the Revolution and amused themselves by shooting at parrots they'd attached to pegs in the beams.[21] In a 1960s renovation of the house, Richard Gachot found iron ammunition balls embedded in the walls. These pieces seemed to confirm the tale about this use of the ammunition.

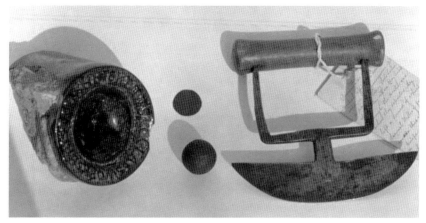

Above: A photograph of artifacts found at the Henry Post House in Westbury. The iron ammunition shot (1⅛-inch diameter ball) can be seen in the center of the photograph. *From* A History of the Henry Post House *by Richard Gachot*.

Left: A photograph of two iron grapeshot ammunition balls found at British/Loyalist troop encampment sites from the Revolutionary War period on Long Island (1–1⅛-inch diameter). *Artifacts from the collection of the author; photograph by the author.*

The Lydia Post diary also mentions stuffed parrots, but they are described as ornaments mounted to the walls in the Pattison (Post) house: "The moment the Hessians took their leave Friend Pattison caused the broken places in the wall to be repaired, for the Colonel's lady had the room ornamented, all around with stuffed parrots, perched on sticks driven in the wall."[22]

This fascinating tale may in fact be just a tale. A history of the Henry Post house written by Richard Gachot includes a photograph of the iron ammunition ball and one of a Hessian/British sword that was also found in the house and has since been made into a chopping knife. The iron ball is noted as being 1⅛ inches in diameter. This author has found similar 1- to 1⅛-inch iron balls at other British encampment sites on Long Island. In each case, the balls were found as lone specimens. The size of the ball found in the Post house and the fact that it is made of iron confirms that the ammunition is not a musket ball but a small artillery projectile known more commonly as grapeshot. Grapeshot was an ammunition cartridge cluster of small iron balls that, when fired from a cannon, would disperse across a field of fire at close range. The fact that these artifacts are found as single balls at encampment and troop housing sites presumes that the balls were probably kept at the Post house as gaming pieces and/or mementoes by the soldiers. It's most likely that the Hessians housed in the Post house were also responsible for creating and ornamenting their space with the stuffed parrots mentioned in the Lydia Post diary. The local history of Long Island attests to the Hessian soldiers being skilled in crafting handiworks and giving them as gifts to children in the region.

Beyond the quartering of private soldiers, high-ranking British officers quartered on Long Island usually had quarters in a house all to themselves. Many times, their quarters were in properties that had been confiscated from Patriot owners who had abandoned their residences. The Patriot colonel Jacob Blackwell had his home in Queens confiscated and marked with a heavily grooved "broad arrow" of the king of England, signifying British ownership. This mark can still be seen in the door that is saved and displayed in the collection of the Greater Astoria Historical Society. After the Battle of Long Island in 1776, Generals William Howe and Henry

Grooved mark of a "broad arrow," on the preserved front door of the original Jacob Blackwell house in Queens, New York. *Photograph by the author, taken at the Greater Astoria Historical Society Museum.*

Clinton set up headquarters in some of the most exquisite homes in Newtown Village on Long Island and in close proximity to New York City. The headquarters were located close to nearby troop encampments and Newtown Creek, which was the wintering haven for the British fleet.[23]

Flatbush and a number of other towns nearby were selected for the billeting of American officers who had been captured at the Battle of Long Island. Instead of being confined to prisons, they were required to give parole and then were sent to board among the families of the county. Congress agreed to pay residents two dollars a week for their boarding.

Red Coat Soldiers Toasting the Ladies of the House. Painting by Howard Pyle, WikiArt.

Colonel Graydon was one of those billeting in Flatbush at the home of Jacob Suydam. He recalled:

> *Room and bed were clean, he relates in his memoirs, but the living rather scanty. What was meant for tea at breakfast he calls a sorry wash; the bread was half baked, because of the scarcity of fuel. A little pickled beef was boiled for dinner when the officers first came; but that gone, clams, called clippers, took its place. For supper they got mush, and skimmed milk and butter milk, with molasses; and this was the food relished best of all, after they became used to it.*[24]

Moving parties of British forces farther out on the island seemed to favor setting up their headquarters in homes of known Patriot sympathizers, some of whom had remained on Long Island and some whom had fled to Connecticut. Samuel Townsend of Oyster Bay, Platt Carll of Dix's Hills, Dr. James Townsend of Jericho, William Downs of Aquebogue and Peter Vail of Southold were all supporters of independence who had their homes used as headquarters for periods by the British army. All of these owners were known signers of the Continental Associations from 1775 and 1776 and/or members of the provincial congresses. William Downs in Aquebogue had to give up his house and move into a smaller house nearby during this period. He was also made an agent and employed by the commander to get provisions for the army.[25] Downs is also listed as a signer of Tryon's list who gave the oath of allegiance to King George III in Southold in 1778.[26] William Downs, among many others who remained on the island, appears to have struggled greatly with the taking of sides and the need for personal safety during the years of occupation.

Larger British winter troop cantonments were established in Jamaica and Flushing on the west end of the island after 1777. General Oliver Delancey, commanding three battalions of Loyalists, set up his headquarters in Jamaica. Farmhouses, barns and churches were used as barracks. The main camps and cantonments of soldiers in Jamaica were set up along present-day Highland Avenue and built into the south-facing hillsides.[27]

In nearby Flushing, British officers set up headquarters along present-day Northern Boulevard, and troop campsites were established along the Black Stump Road. The Black Stump Road, being an important route for linking British positions, had troops encamped on the farms of the Hooglands, Brinckerhoffs and Bownes. Farther north, on the Pigeon Meadow Road, Hessians quartered at the Duryee and Lawrence farms.[28]

Farther out on Long Island, the British and Hessians quartered in farmhouses stretching from Herricks Village in the west to Norwich and

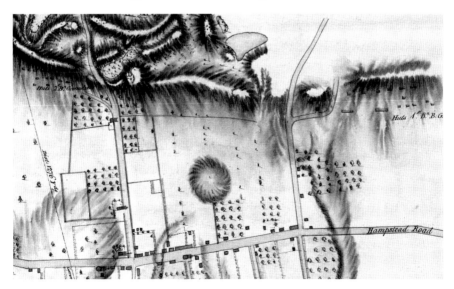

A Map of the Pass at Jamaica, Long Island (1782). Troop huts can be seen at the top right and top left set into the hillsides. *Courtesy of the William L. Clements Library, University of Michigan in Ann Arbor, Michigan.*

Hut Camp of the 17th Regiment of Foot, Inwood Hill, New York City (1915), by John Ward Dunsmore. Courtesy of the New York Historical Society.

Jericho in the east. An enemy report from January 1779 states that "estimating the Hessian Regt Jagers, infantry of Cathcart Legion (British Legion), Queens Rangers or Simcoe's as per margin together, are 1,980 Strong."[29] Huntington and Lloyd's Neck farther to the east became important British headquarters, with British and Loyalist troops continually posted in the area. Cantonments of both British and Loyalist soldiers encircled the southern ridges of Lloyd's Neck and all the areas near Fort Franklin.

British military engineers established cantonments and encampments, taking advantage of the natural landscape. Buildings were oriented to maximize the natural light and warmth they brought in. Huts in Newtown in Queens County were constructed in a large configuration, with the huts being fifty feet long and rectangular in form. The entrances of the huts were open to the south to admit the sun's rays, their roofs were thatched and their three sides were sodded up to the eaves to keep off the north-west wind.[30]

Captain John Peebles of the grenadier company of the Forty-Second (Royal Highland) Regiment of Foot described winter huts that were being constructed in Jamaica, Queens County, Long Island, in 1778 for the British grenadier battalions:

> *The Ground for the huts being mark'd out in the morng. on the So: side of the hill north of Town, the men with the few tools they had, broke ground & fell to work to make huts for their abode in Winter, each hut 24 feet by 12 to contain 12 men the wall partly dug in the face of the hill, and the rest made up of sod, the roof to be covered with cedar branches & thin sod— they all front the South & are sheltered from the No. winds by the ridge.*[31]

In the archaeological research of William Calver and Reginald Bolton of the early twentieth century, a winter cantonment was uncovered and studied in northern Manhattan in New York City. Based on their research, they reconstructed a typical hut at the Dyckman farmhouse in New York City in 1915. In this reconstruction, they moved an original stone floor, walls and fireplace from a dug hut site and added timbers to create the full reconstruction. This hut originally would have housed six to eight soldiers.[32]

Hut sites in the New York and Long Island areas were all located in close proximity to ample sources of water. The permanently occupied cantonments that were built in the Dutch Kills area of Newtown, Long Island, used the waters of the "Wolf Swamp." The writings of Skillman about the Dutch Kills area mentions, "The old well first experienced the military occupation, the soldiers in their madness after water quickly broke the bucket ropes and then descended by the aid of spikes driven into the side of the well, and the water was handed up by relays of men until the supply was exhausted."[33] The swamp water source became an important reason why the area was constantly occupied throughout the Revolution.

The research and writings of Calver and Bolton have added greatly to our present knowledge of the daily lives of soldiers during this period. Their

The Hessian hut (reconstructed soldier's headquarters) at Dyckman House, Broadway and West 204th Street, New York City, 1916. *Courtesy of the New York Historical Society.*

The Fire-Place in the Hut (circa 1916). An interior view of the reconstructed Hessian military hut at the Dyckman Farmhouse Museum. *From the Reginald Pelham Bolton Scrapbook, Collection of the Dyckman Farmhouse Museum.*

studies of British hut sites in the New York City area found similarities in the identifications of other sites of similar character within the region. They found at most sites regimental buttons and military equipage. The personal equipment of troops was found intermixed with meat bones, oyster shells, broken rum bottles, pottery ironware and barrel hoops.[34] The hoops were probably from casks of British army provisions. This author's own analysis of cantonment sites in the Lloyd Neck area attests to similar findings at hut sites. Meat bones, barrel hoops, iron strapping and fragments of wine and rum bottles have been found. Oyster shell beds are also commonly found at these sites. Oysters and shellfish seem to have been a significant part of a soldier's diet on Long Island.

Encampments and troop quarters were, on several occasions, set up in churches and churchyards. Many of these churchyards were cleared of trees and located on heights, providing good camping grounds. The experience of camping in a graveyard cannot be assumed to have been enjoyable for most of the soldiery, as most had fears and feelings of uneasiness within these surroundings.[35]

These long periods of encampment gave ample time for the soldiery to have many working and free hours. Their daily work tasks included collecting wood and supplies, building and repairing huts and fortifications and performing daily camp hygiene and upkeep. Soldiers also had many free hours in which they were able to rest and/or take part in some form of entertainment. The private soldiers, it appears, played many card and board games. The number of lead and iron artifacts cut in many shapes and sizes that are found underground at these sites today attest to this. Officers indulged in greater amusements, sometimes fox hunting, shooting game and playing in cricket matches, cards and music.[36]

2

REQUISITION

etween 1777 and 1781, Long Island and its population suffered greatly as the British requisitioned supplies. Failures in British supply chains and the growing needs of the troops stationed in New York City exacerbated the situation. The supplies available in Queens County in villages such as Newtown, Flushing and Jamaica were not enough. The British army needed cordwood for fuel and transportation facilities, such as horses, wagons, carts, drivers and stables, along with food for the horses in the form of straw and oats.[37] All of these items were regularly requisitioned from private citizens during this time. The acquisition of these supplies was to follow a system of requisition and payment supervised by parties of soldiers collecting goods from local sources and putting them into stores. Property owners were to receive vouchers redeemable for cash.[38] Long Island being an island meant it was a somewhat secure source of resources, and it allowed for a more linear supply chain from east to west using its roads and waterways. A form of martial law was essentially established by the British occupiers between 1779 and 1781 on Long Island.[39]

By the fall of 1778, areas of western Long Island became significant points of immediate supply resources that could be quickly accumulated and transferred to New York. Magazines, which were, in the eighteenth century, essentially storehouses, were used for the collection of supply. Most of these storehouses would have been existing farmyards, woodyards or barn buildings requisitioned for this use. In Hempstead, a magazine was set up for horse stabling and for the collection of supplies in the center of town near the Sammis Tavern.

> *The Horses stood on poles laid lengthwise, or on sand daily renewed. The wood-yard and hay magazine were north of Sammis's Inn, enclosed and guarded. There were to be seen numerous long stacks of hay, containing 100 or 200 loads. The wood or hay was inspected as the farmers brought it in, and certificates given, payable at the Forage Office, N.Y.*[40]

Jericho, another village farther east became a key point of collection and transfer early in the war. In an espionage letter from Samuel Culper to Benjamin Tallmadge in December 1778, Culper described the British supply situation on Long Island:

> *The Packet and Cork Fleet that hath bene a long time expected is not yet arrived and Should they fail they would be in a most deplorable Situation, their provisions I assure you are very Short, their forage here goes like the dew it Cannot last them half the Winter. Lord Cathcart's Legion at Jerico is the reception of all.*[41]

Jericho in 1778 was a camp position of the British Legion (also known as Cathcart's Legion), which was a combined provincial infantry and cavalry unit. The village housed a storehouse magazine.[42] Legion troopers aided in the quick movement and collection of supplies on the island. A storage magazine was also established at the village of Oyster Bay. That village was under the command of Colonel John Graves Simcoe of the Queen's Rangers.[43] Between Jericho and Oyster Bay, supplies were transferred to shipping at the docks of Oyster Bay and then moved by water to New York City. Other magazine storehouses were also set up within the area: "Capt Daniel Youngs is ordered to furnish fourteen Waggons with Horses & Drivers to the same for the Purpose of Carting Forage for the Magazien at Hempstead and Herricks from Smithtown."[44]

Orders given to the Queens County militia from William Tryon at Jamaica in 1779 discuss the requisitioning of the inhabitants:

> *To Capt. Daniel Youngs, Capt. Queen Co. Militia*
> *REGULATIONS for the Captains of Militia, and Justices of the Peace in Queens County.*

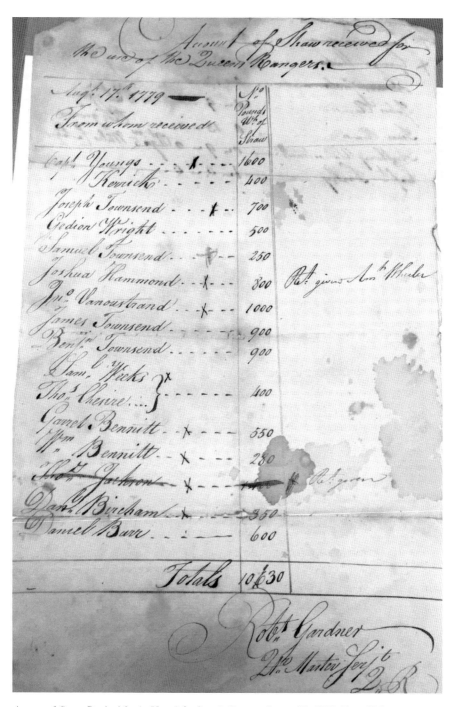

Account of Straw Received for the Use of the Queen's Rangers, August 17, 1779. From Hofstra University's Long Island Studies Institute, Nassau County Museum Reference Collection.

The King's Troops cantoned in each district in Queen's County, are to be supplied with Fuel by the inhabitants of the neighborhood.

The Captain of Militia and Justice of the Peace, living in the same district to join in assessing on the inhabitants of the Beat, the requisite quantity of Wood. Those who have no woodlands, and are of ability, will furnish with proportion.

In those districts in which any Troops are hutted, the inhabitants by the direction of the Captain of Militia, to cart the Wood to the common Wood-Yard, and to unload as ordered by the Barrack-Master or Quarter-Master of the Regiment in his absence: But where the troops are cantoned, or billeted on the inhabitants, the Captains of Militia so to regulate the matter, that each inhabitant may supply the nearest fire. The whole in the district nevertheless to bear an equal proportion, in the quantity requisite by assessment.

Such Waggons and Horses as may from time to time be wanted by the Commissary General or Barrack Master General's departments, or by the Commanding Officers of Corps on emergency for the purpose of carting Provisions. Forage, Fuel, or Baggage, are also to be supplied by the Captain of Militia, who will regulate this service with all possible equality among the inhabitants who have teams in their respective districts.[45]

Those who did not comply were issued fines; the same regulations state, "And every inhabitant who shall pay neglect or disobedience to the order of the Captain of his district for the purpose of the afore-mentioned, will be fined according to the degree of neglect or offense."[46]

A similar request was issued by the British commanders for manpower and supplies for fortification building on Long Island in October 1779:

A requisition having been made to Gen. Delancey, of L.I. Militia, to furnish 500 men, to parade with their blankets on Aug. 23, to march for Brooklyn, to be employed in repairing and constructing new works there; 210 of which were to be from Suffolk County, who were also to furnish and send to the magazine at Brooklyn, 5,000 fascines, 9 ft. long, and stripped of leaves; 25,000 pickets, from 3 to 4 ft. long; 5,000 fraisings or stockades, from 9 to 10 ft. long, and 6 to 8 in. thick; 5,000 railing of 6 or 7 ft.[47]

With the inhabitants refusing to comply, a threat was issued by the command:

Sir: You will signify to the people of Suffolk Co. that if the requisition is not immediately complied with a detachment of troops will be sent into the district, and every person who shall refuse shall be turned out of L.I., and their farms will be all for the support of those who have suffered from real attachment to Government. Rawdon, Ad. Gen.[48]

The army confiscated everything from crops, wood, victuals, rum, household items and even clothing. At first, wood and confiscations were taken from the lands of absentee rebels who had left the island.[49] Then the local inhabitants were requested to turn over their property to the army. British officials were supposed to provide receipts for the goods. When receipts were issued, the holders were rarely compensated.[50]

Stories abound of supplies that were taken without credit given. Timothy Carll in Huntington listed the following:

September 16th 1776 my oxen was drove to Newton by Gen. Delanceys orders, which I valued at twenty five pounds, November 20 1777 my teame was taken to carry baggage from Huntington to Jamaica by order of Colonel Cruger, January 22, 1779 aparty of troops that was going to Southampton to Sir William Erskine came to my house kept eighteen horses to fresh hay one night four bushels & ½ of oates, March 27th 1779 Leit. Moffit came to my house Rations for twelve horses and took five bushels of oates, About the 20th of October 1779 Colonel Dalton was out o aparty of pleashure and graining and came to my house and took a cow out of my pastur that cost twenty four pounds no pay for none of the above.[51]

Beyond what the individual inhabitants could supply, it seems that greater quantities of resources were demanded of more significant landholders or groups. Platt Carll in Dix Hills, whose property will be discussed further, was requisitioned many times throughout the war:

Jany. 10 1777—Rec'd of Mr. Platt Carll three Hundred weight of English Hay for the use of the Commisary Gen'll, 1 Pound 4s.

Dicks Hills, ye 10th May 1781—Rec'd from Platt Carll Oats for one of the Quarter Master General, and five of the Seventeenth of Dragoons, Horses, Detached with me on his Majestys Service. 6s.

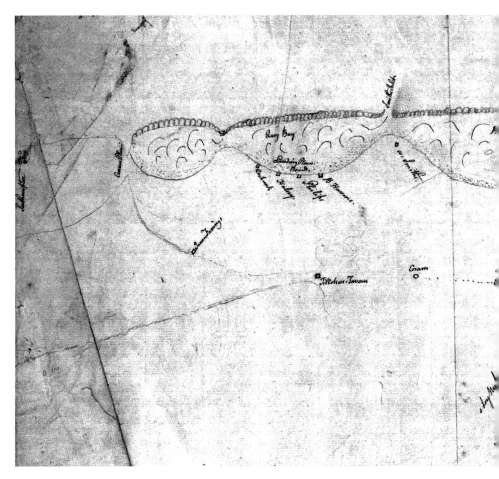

Part of the southwestern shore of Long Island. *Courtesy of the William L. Clements Library, University of Michigan in Ann Arbor, Michigan.*

Dick Hills 22ⁿᵈ Jan'y 1782—Rec'd of Platt Carll, ten Rations of Tope stalks for the Queens County Brigade Horses now emp'd Carting Forage For the Com'y Gen'l. 10s.[52]

In nearby Smithtown, an account book kept by the Society of Smithtown stating claims against King George III lists a significant claim of 127 pounds 18 shillings 4 pence for 6,396 feet of boards at 20 pounds 8 shillings per thousand taken from out of the Presbyterian church in November 1778. The notation says, "The above boards were of the best pine and taken for the use of the Government by Colonel Tarleton and Major Cochran."[53]

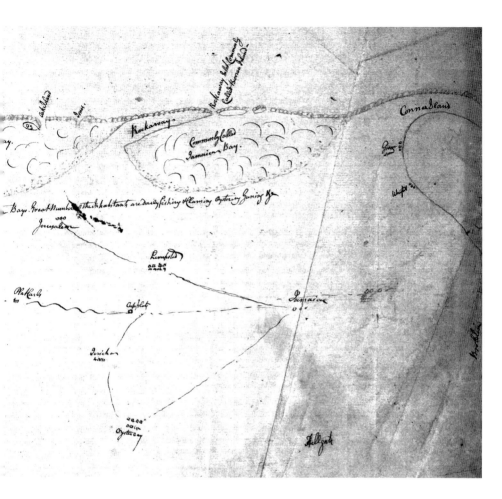

The continued requisitioning of supplies, such as wood collection, led to a dwindling of resources over time. To ensure the British had complete knowledge of all the materials available, a census was taken in 1781. On the basis of the census, supplies were requisitioned according to the colonists' ability to provide them.[54]

An order by Captain Daniel Youngs to Seargent William Bennet from Oyster Bay in September 1781 states:

> *To Sgt. Wm. Bennit I received orders from the police office of the 31st of Jan. to make a regular white return of all the inhabitants both the men and women and children white and black horses stock carts wagons hay and grain of all sort and you are required to go round and take a particular count of all beginning at your house and so to Richard Weckes so to Mutton*

town and taking all on the west side of the road to Benjamin Townsend
and take an account of all the acres of woodland. Each man has and bring
an account to me by Sunday morning so I may be able to make a general
one of the whole.[55]

There is an informative map of Long Island within the papers of Sir
Henry Clinton from 1778–79 that shows locations all the way from Brooklyn
in the western part of the island to Southampton on the east end. On
viewing the map, a path between separate points seems to denote a linear
connection that may have been the main route of travel and supply for the
British forces. On analyzing the possible owners of the properties on the
map and their histories, the locations seem to demonstrate locations that
may have allowed safe passage and/or friendly supply and refreshment for
the movement of the British forces and their supplies. The histories of these
locations also demonstrate the complexity of ownership in a time of war,
with many properties having been forfeited or confiscated by those more
loyal to the British cause.

On the map, Long Island is portrayed upsidedown. The top of the map
in fact shows the south shore of Long Island. Starting at Brooklyn on the
right side of the map, there is a fork of routes shown. One route is shown
heading south to Hempstead and then on to Jerusalem (present-day Wantagh)
on the south shore. Similarly, there is a northern route noted to Oyster Bay
and another to Oyster Bay by way of Jericho. The central route stretches the
island, beginning with a point noted as "CaptPlats" or "EaphPlats." It took
some research to find what this location is, but it seems this may have been the
residence of Captain Jesse Platt, a veteran of the New York provincial troops
from 1759 to 1761, first as a lieutenant and then as a captain, who served in
the French and Indian War. A pair of deeds from 1763 refer to a fifty-acre
property "whereon Jesse Platt now lives."[56] The land was bounded on one side
by Old Country Road near Hempstead in an area named Clovesville, which
is near present-day Mineola. Platt had passed away in 1769, but it seems the
property may have remained in the family. His former prominence in the
British service may have made the property a stopover for the British in the
Revolution. The accuracy of this conjecture on the location is not certain.

The second position marked on the map is certainly that of the Platt
Carll Inn in Dix Hills in South Huntington. The Platt Carll Inn is recorded
as being occupied by the British during the war, and it was a sort of general
headquarters for the central area of the island. Historian Henry C. Platt
maintained that "the British forces often marched there and made it their

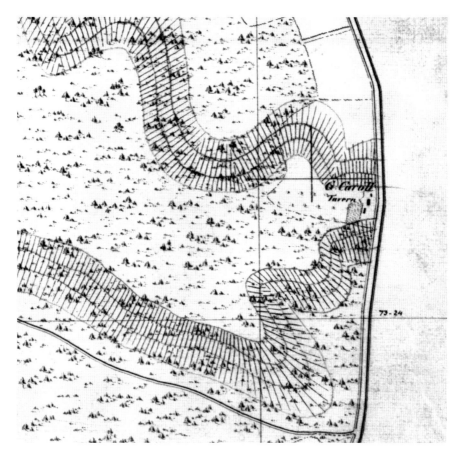

A section of an early map showing the area of the Platt Carll Tavern along the Jericho Turnpike. From a map of the Harbor and Village of Huntington, North Shore of Long Island, 1837. *Courtesy of the University Libraries Digital Research Collections, Stony Brook University.*

stopping place, on their foraging excursions."[57] The inn and homestead of the Carll family stood at the top of a hill on the north side of Jericho Turnpike and faced south. An extra team of animals was often needed to haul heavy stagecoaches up to the inn. The inn was also a place where public meetings were held and where the local militia drilled.[58]

A story from the Revolutionary period survives that says the British hoped to collect possessions reportedly stored in the house from Patriot raiding parties. To force Platt Carll to reveal the location of these items, the British put a rope around his neck and drew him up in the air several times. Carll never revealed the location. He was taken to a prison ship in Wallabout Bay in New York and incarcerated.[59] We can only assume the inn was then considered confiscated property for most of the war. The inn is long gone today, but a house from 1795, which replaced the original Carll home, remains on the property.

The location on the map noted as Smithtown would be the historic town of Smithtown today. British troops and officers frequented the inn of Epinetus Smith, which was located on the main street of the town.[60] In the Blydenburgh Manuscripts, there are articles that were furnished for services rendered and for items requisitioned to a number of influential British and Loyalist commanders of the war in Smithtown.

The next town marked on the map heading east is Coram. Coram was an ancient town located in the middle of the island in the town of Brookhaven. It was the seat of government for the town of Brookhaven during the Revolution. In 1775 and again in early 1776, the committee of safety for Brookhaven met in Coram, with several landowners of the town being present.[61] By 1780, Coram had become a camp and a significant storage location for three hundred tons of hay for the British army. The Queen's Rangers are recorded to have collected the hay from the area of Miller Place in northern Brookhaven.[62] The hay was burned by American forces in November 1780 after their successful attack of Fort St. George.

A photograph of the Epenetus Smith Tavern as it appears today in Smithtown. The dormers were added in 1911. *Photograph by the author.*

East of Coram is a position noted as Tillotson's Tavern. After researching the name and its historical location, the conjecture is that the noted tavern is the historical location of the former Long Island House in present-day Riverhead on Long Island. Before Riverhead was known by this name, it was called River Head. It was the site of the first county courthouse of Suffolk County. In 1750, John Griffing bought a farm estimated at 130 acres from Thomas Fanning close to the county courthouse. Griffing kept an inn and tavern known then as the Griffing Inn.[63]

In researching the name Tillotson, it appears that Samuel Tillotson had moved from Smithtown to Southold in late 1775 or early 1776, and for a time, he occupied John Griffing's property in Aquebogue Village.[64] John Griffing had taken refuge in Connecticut at the start of the war. Samuel Tillotson is listed as signing Governor Tryon's 1778 oath of allegiance for Southold. The map portrays the name Tillotson, as he was most likely the inn and tavern keeper in the early years of the Revolutionary War. The Griffing Tavern and Inn later became the Long Island House. An article in the *County Review* in 1924 notes that a local historian, George A. Buckingham, wrote an article, stating, "There are many interesting stories and legends connected with this veritably ancient property. It is pretty well authenticated, however, that a wandering squad of British cavalry bivouacked there during the War of the Revolution and stabled their horses in the public room."[65]

The next location noted on the map is James Fanning's property. This was the land of James Decker Fanning II in present-day Flanders, Long Island. He was the son of James Fanning I, an early pioneer of the River Head town and a veteran captain in the British service during the French and Indian War. James Fanning II of Flanders had a brother named Thomas Fanning, noted above and formerly of Riverhead, who, during the Revolution, remained loyal to the British Crown, attaining the rank of captain in the "King's American Regiment of Foot," which had been organized by his other brother Colonel Edmund Fanning.[66] They also had a brother named Phineas Fanning who fought for the Patriot side. Due to overwhelming family loyalties to the king, the Fanning property in Flanders was most likely a position marked as friendly to the British cause and popular stopover point.

The Canoe Place is noted on the map close to the top left corner. An early colonial house on the main road between Riverhead and Southampton at the Canoe Place became an inn for travelers. During the Revolutionary War, it housed British army officers, who set up the inn as a headquarters.[67] Behind the inn on a rising height of ground, the British also built a redoubt fortification that became known as the Fort at Canoe Place.

A view looking north across the Peconic River to the first county courthouse in River Head. Reproduced from an early woodcut. *Courtesy of Dover Publications Inc.*

The last location marked on the extreme left end of the map is the village of Southampton. During the war, Southampton became the headquarters of the British forces of the eastern district of Long Island. In 1778 and 1779, there was a significant increase in the number of troops in the area, due largely to the fact that the French alliance with the American army had been signed in February 1779 and a large French fleet was anchored east of Long Island in Newport, Rhode Island.[68] In February 1779, fourteen companies of light infantry, or seven hundred men, were quartered in Southampton, and this number grew to four thousand shortly after.[69] Southampton, Sag Harbor and Sagg Village also provided significant foraging resources for the British that were carried back to New York and western Long Island.

Not noted on the map were the villages that also populated the north fork of eastern Long Island. This fork of land was also part of the network of towns that supplied and reinforced the north shore of Long Island. Just past Riverhead, toward the north fork, was the village of Aquebogue, which was an important farming area and early settlement. There are records of the British requisitioning the house of William Downs of Aquebogue for use as a headquarters. It is certain that troops were also encamped close to this position for periods of time.

Farther to the east, the village of Mattituck is recorded as serving as a troop encampment position for British units moving to the east end under

William Tryon in the summer of 1778.[70] The homestead of Deacon Thomas Reeve was used as headquarters for the officers.[71] The village of Southold was also subsequently occupied by a force of five hundred foot soldiers and fifty cavalrymen (dragoons). Tryon's headquarters in Southold was located in the confiscated house of Peter Vail, who was a Patriot refugee serving in the American army.[72]

3

PLUNDERING

Hand in hand with requisitioning during the war came the problem of plundering by individuals on both sides. Opportunistic soldiers preyed on anything that could be eaten or sold for money and easily taken. Plundering was outside the rules of the requisitioning system and was outright stealing done by the troops, usually those lower down in the ranks. The encampments and cantonments of Long Island were inhabited by soldiers with voracious appetites for firewood, livestock, poultry and vegetables. It was not only the British soldiers who took part in the plundering but also German and Loyalist soldiers, army wives, civilians employed as wagon drivers, artificers and other camp followers.[73]

To the British commander General Sir William Howe, plundering was prohibited and criticized on the grounds that it was likely to estrange loyal or potentially friendly Americans. He ordered his troops to act as liberators, not as conquerors. Howe later defended himself after the war by arguing before Parliament that he had issued a series of proclamations against such misbehavior.[74] After Howe's command, General Sir Henry Clinton made similar efforts to minimize plundering. He recognized "that anything less was not only militarily unwise and morally reprehensible but also likely to be politically damaging."[75]

Examples of plundering abound in the histories of Long Island. In the writings of Skillman about the encampments of soldiers in the Dutch Kills area of Newtown in Queens County, he mentioned, "In a plot of Woodland near this encampment, belonging to Mr. Albertis they had many Barrels

The Residence of David Twining 1787 (1847), Edward Hicks. The painting shows the resources of a typical colonial homestead. *From WikiArt.*

and Casks sunk in the ground where they secreted stolen things."[76] It seems that articles needed for the war effort were accumulated by all means and stored throughout the cantonments. A local inhabitant recalled that when he was eleven or twelve years old, several incidents of stealing took place in Newtown. One night his father lost an entire litter of pigs; he inquired about them but could find no record of them.[77]

Many individuals in the village of Huntington were also forcibly robbed. Ezra Conkling, who lived in the eastern part of the village, suffered greatly at the hands of the British, who stole almost everything eatable from his farm. He eventually hid and fed a fat calf for himself in his milk room. The story is that he had a Tory neighbor whose daughters flirted with local British officers and told them where the calf was hidden. Several informed British soldiers later came to the house early one morning under the pretense of searching for a deserter. In the upstairs area of the house, they threw two of the children of Mr. Conkling out of their beds and cut the bed ropes, stating they had found a deserter downstairs in the milk room and wanted some rope to tie him up.[78]

A story from the Lydia Post diary tells of similar plundering by small groups. The story is told by an acquaintance of the author:

> *A family living a mile from us were quietly sitting together in the evening, when a noise was heard at the door like that of a sharp instrument thrust into it. On opening the door, there stood a red-coat with his sabre in his hand, which he had struck into the wood an inch or two. He was backed by a dozen men. They pushed their way in, and were very unruly, rummaging and ransacking every drawer and closet; but the family had long before taken the precaution to place all their valuables and money in a small room, which opened out of the common sitting room, putting a large cupboard before the door, which was covered so entirely; so that the Hessians quartered there last winter never discovered the existence of the room. A cunning device. The red-coats, highly enraged at finding nothing, began to threaten terrible things if they did not divulge the hiding place.*[79]

There is a story in which Joel and Zophar Rogers of Elwood Road in Northport were hanged by the British, who then continuously requested the locations of their hidden goods and money. Not giving into the demands of the British, the men were left hanging to die. One of the brothers managed to loosen the rope around his neck and free his brother. Escaping with their lives, they went back to their house and found their money safe in a pair of old shoes, where they had hidden it.[80]

Repeated stories abide of perpetrators terrorizing the local citizenry by hanging them by their necks for a while and then cutting them down just before they passed out. Certain individuals were tortured in this way two or three times. It can only be assumed that this type of torture was utilized for the interrogation of individuals who were suspected of hiding valuables in their households.

To evade plunder, local inhabitants took to hiding their valuables. During the war, bands of British troops were known to stop and demand dinner from known sympathizers of the American cause. Troops stopped at the home of Major Leek in Middle Island, and Mrs. Leek was requested to provide dinner for the party. While the dinner was being prepared, one of the soldiers, whom Mrs. Leek assumed to be an officer, went around the dining room, hitting the sides of the walls with his sword to see if there were any secret panels that may be discovered. The soldier was not able to find anything. Years later, the story of a secret panel in the house did come to light. A descendant of the Leeks who was staying at the house and knew the story of the British coming to the home was able to find a secret panel with a cupboard and valuables hidden behind it.[81]

Similarly, in nearby Miller Place, both sympathizers and common inhabitants took the best precautions they could to save their possessions from British seizure and plunder from both sides of the conflict. Local women stowed away their silk gowns and valuables in trunks and boxes that could be pushed out of sight under the eaves of their attics. Captain Solomon Davis, being a very wealthy man of the town, took his gold to a field behind his house and buried it, marking the spot with a large rock. Captain Davis was killed during the war. The hidden valuables were never recovered, and a century or so later, Horace Hudson, who then owned the land, found about £500 sterling buried at the spot marked with the large rock.[82]

In mid-February 1779, a corporal and five privates, all grenadiers of the Seventy-First Regiment, left their quarters in Sag Harbor at night and went to a local home, asking for water. The homeowners directed them to the well, but the soldiers forced their way into the house. While the corporal stood watch outside, the invaders beat the man of the house and stole their clothing, bedding, leather and a gun. One of the men agreed to testify against the others, and a court-martial found them all guilty of robbery. The man who broke down the door for the others was sentenced to death, and the remaining men were sentenced to receive 1,500 lashes.[83]

An interesting story was recorded in Smithtown in which the local farmers at the time had a place where they hid their cattle from roving British troops. They called it Yorke, and when asked by the British occupiers where their livestock had gone, they declared that it had been "taken to Yorke," which was then the common name for New York. But Yorke to them was actually a deep natural glacial kettle hole near Joshua's Path Road between present-day Smithtown and Islip. The town's livestock were hidden in this natural feature, and the site became known as the farmers' Yorke and was so deep that tall trees growing in the hole barely reached the rim.[84] Few know of this place or the story of its significance.

The history of soldiers who were caught plundering is not well documented. The penalty for the crime was capital punishment, and the most common form given was lashings. Early in the capture of New York, in August 1776, the commander in chief observed that "plundering is become so excessive that Commanding Officers of Corps must be responsible that the Soldiers do not quit their Encampments unless upon Duty in which case the Officer Commanding must be answerable for the behavior of his Men."[85] Later, the provost marshal received orders to execute on the spot soldiers found

British soldiers plundering an American colonial home, 1700s. *Wikimedia Commons.*

guilty of marauding. Muster rolls were frequently called, and any soldier found more than a mile from his post would be confined. Only a few troops were actually brought to trial on Long Island. One conviction of these trials sentenced the guilty soldier to one thousand lashes.[86]

Most army offenses committed during the American Revolution were stealing, plundering, robbery and the like.[87] From the fall of 1778 to the summer of 1782, twenty-one British soldiers were tried by the general courts for crimes committed against Long Island inhabitants. The offenses involved livestock theft, housebreaking, robbery, harm to others and murder. There were many more crimes of which the perpetrators were not caught and for which no trials occurred.[88]

4

ABUSES

The residents of Long Island lived in fear of plunder by ragtag units of soldiers, and they also had to suffer through many forms of physical and emotional abuse during the Revolution. At the beginning of the war, 60 percent of the male population on Long Island were neutral and took no sides in the conflict, but as one British officer observed, "We planted an irrecoverable hatred wherever we went, which neither time nor measures will be able to eradicate."[89] One British officer argued that "we should (whenever we get further into the country) give free liberty to the soldiers to ravage it at will, that these infatuated wretches may feel what a calamity war is."[90] Unfortunately, British officers had failed to reconcile with the Long Island population after the capture of the New York City area. Officers of lower rank and privates could not tell Patriots from Loyalists and began abusing all as rebels. Another British officer remarked, "Those poor unhappy wretches who had remained in their habitation through necessity or loyalty were immediately judged…to be Rebels, neither their clothing or property spared, but in the most inhuman and barbarous manner torn from them."[91] Oppression was made possible because martial law was in force, and civilians had no means of bringing suits against military personnel who abused them.[92]

Even General William Howe instructed the owners of cattle who were taken by American forces and collected before the battle of Long Island to present a claim and affirm their loyalty in order to recover their animals. In some cases, a claimant who did as instructed did not get their cattle returned. Some cattle were kept for the army's use with compensation promised, but the payment was never received. The commissaries then billed the government for the cattle, and officials kept the money for themselves. Commissary officials also had inhabitants sign blank receipts under threat of nonpayment. The sums were then inflated and charged to the British government.[93] These types of abuses encouraged inhabitants to view the British as their enemy.

The Presbyterian and Congregational churches also suffered as a whole on Long Island. The reputation of Patriotism among Presbyterian ministers and congregations made them targets for British retribution. The British simply considered Presbyterian church buildings "rebel meetinghouses." Many Presbyterian buildings on Long Island were taken by the occupying forces and used as barracks for troops or for the storage and stabling of horses. Some were taken down completely for the reuse of their materials. The British abused Presbyterian ministers, suspended religious services and scattered congregations. Many ministers were driven away or imprisoned and died.[94]

The Presbyterian Church of South Haven had many famous Patriots within its membership. Colonel William Floyd, Colonel Nathaniel Woodhull and Captain Josiah Smith all attended the church under the leadership of the well-known doctor, reverend and Patriot David Rose. Meetings were held at the church in 1774 in support of the Continental Congress and provincial congresses and the committees of safety and correspondence. After the British occupation, these Patriot leaders, including the reverend, were forced to become refugees in Connecticut. All services in the church were stopped for seven years. The South Haven church became a target for scorn and abuse by the British invaders. Its benches and pulpit were thrown out, and the church was used as a barracks for the British troops and possibly as a stable or hay storage for cavalry horses.[95] Most likely, the occupiers were members of a troop of the Queen's Rangers who were also posted at nearby Coram.

An interesting anecdote from the time of the British use of the South Haven church comes from a descendant of William Floyd, written in 1897:

> *The Present church of the Presbyterian Parish at So'Haven occupies the site of the church built in 1740, rebuilt in 1828, which was used by the British Soldiers as a stable for their horses, and on one of the sides the building was riddled with bullet holes-where in practicing with their muskets the Soldiers had not always hit the bulls-eye.*[96]

It is not known if this story is true. A written history of the South Haven church states that timbers and boards from the 1740 church were reused in the rebuilt 1828 church.[97]

The wartime situation on the island also made travel by individuals very dangerous. Stories of abuse by British soldiers fueled concern for movement on Long Island. In the Post diary, a story of a countryman says that a traveler was met along the road by a company of English soldier ruffians who began swearing and threatening the individual if they did not say, "God save the king." The traveler refused to do so, thinking the challenge was just a threat. One of the aggressive soldiers stepped up to the traveler with a drawn sword. He

A view of the South Haven Presbyterian Church from an antique postcard. *From the collection of the author.*

managed to keep brandishing the sword as he shouted, "Say it or—you're a dead man!" The villain paused a minute; the threatened man continued to be silent, and the threat was put into execution.[98]

Similarly, the Post diary tells a story of robbers who, in 1780, entered the house of John Willis and were so exasperated at finding no booty that they tied the hands of every family member behind their backs, along with those of a guest preacher, who was staying with them. They dragged the wife of Mr. Willis about the house by her hair and then left, telling the family that they had set fire to the house. As the flames kindled, their hands remained tied.[99]

A story of Goldsmith Davis of Coram tells of similar abuses taking place at his household. Goldsmith Davis was a man of wealth, and on hearing that the British were pillaging in his area, he hid his family in the woods for safety. He stayed to guard his home. The British came to his house and overpowered him, taking him to his attic garret and hanging him from the rafters, where he was bayoneted and left to die. After the British left, his family came out of hiding and cut him down. Supposedly, his bleeding wound left stains on the floorboards for many years, marking the spot where he was tortured in the house.[100]

The story of Goldsmith Davis's hanging in a house is not the only one of its kind recorded. Onderdonk wrote, "A body of armed men with fixed bayonets, came to the house of Gilbert and Simon Fleet, near Huntington, and robbed the 2 families of all the money and plate they could find, and had nigh strangled one of them by hanging him up to a beam in his kitchen."[101]

Another story of torture says that soldiers of the King's American Regiment entered the house of Willet Browne near the Black Stump Road in Flushing at night. They tied him to a bedpost and tortured him by holding a candle to the tips of his fingers to induce him to tell them where his money was hidden.[102]

Another form of physical abuse that was used by the British army on the inhabitants on Long Island was recorded in a post-Revolution extract published in the *New York Journal* of 1810. The following quote is taken from part of the observations noted regarding the act of picquetting, which was a quite common form of punishment performed by the British army. Picquetting was a military punishment usually reserved for the enlisted soldier who disobeyed military orders. It appears to have been popular among the cavalrymen of the time. The following story tells of this torture being used on a civilian.

> *A number of horsemen of the 16th and 17th regiment of dragoons, being quartered in the neighbourhood of Jericho, on Long Island; some of the men charged one of the inhabitants, a blacksmiths by trade, (named Jacob Williams) with welding his own tongs, to prevent their being used by them—but even this charge was destitute of truth, the fact was that the smiths, er farriers, belonging to the troops, had worked them up into shoes for their own horses. For the above alledged offence, without any investigation, one of the captains ordered that Williams should be picquetted. Accordingly he was immediately taken into Elias Hick's orchard, where his right hand and left leg being first tied together behind him, he was suspended by the wrist of the other arm, with a cord, to the limb of an apple tree; without any thing to rest his right (bare) foot on but a peg of hard wood placed in the ground under him, merely as an aggravation, the upperend being so sharp that he could bear no weight on it. In this manner he was kept till he fainted—he was then let down, but not before nature was so far exhausted that it was some time doubtful whether he could be restored to life: he at length, however, revived and was discharged.[103]*

Sadly, the offense rendered the individual's hand useless for a long time. He had a large family who was entirely dependent on his support.

Luisa Calderón being tortured, as illustrated in one of the many prints at the time. Unknown author, 1806. *Wikimedia Commons.*

The quartering of troops in private homes and outbuildings also made the possibility of disease and the spread of smallpox a constant threat. The presence of soldiers in an area also brought the reality of rape and venereal disease to communities. It has been reported that the British soldiers "attacked pregnant women, the elderly, and girls as young as thirteen years old, and sometimes gang raped their victims over the course of several days."[104]

By 1780, the British falsely claimed they had fulfilled their pledge to restore civil authority. In July 1780, Major General James Robertson, acting as governor of New York, appointed George Duncan Ludlow as superintendent to a newly created court of police on Long Island. Ludlow was a local resident, and Robertson claimed the court of police acted as a partial restoration of civil government on the island. The court saw cases and legal disputes local to Long Island. The pledge to have civil authority, however, was taken in vain. Ludlow was a New York Supreme Court justice before the war, and the court of police represented nothing more than a different version of martial law. Trial by jury was not restored, and local justices lost their power to try small matters.[105]

Thomas Jones, a strong Loyalist on Long Island, requested that civil courts be opened. Jones believed that the courts were not opened because "barrack-masters, quarter-masters, and commissaries would have been prosecuted, and punished for plunder, robberies and other illegal acts."[106]

Another terrible story of assault and its retribution can be seen in the plundering and violent attack on Parmenas Jackson of Jerusalem, Long Island. Seven men attacked him on January 10, 1781, and he was fatally wounded. They locked away his family and demanded his money. After Jackson refused to relinquish its location, the attackers hacked him terribly on his head and arm as he tried to ward of the blows. Reports after the attack record that the wall overhead was spotted with blood. He was left to die. The doctors who attended Mr. Jackson were recalled to have taken pieces of his skull off to relieve the pressure on his brain. His brain was exposed so that its motions were visible during the procedure. He survived only nine days. One of the robbers was recorded in the story as John DeGraw. Supposedly, a servant girl who worked for Mr. Jackson was a brother to DeGraw, who was a soldier in Delancey's Third Battalion. After the attack, he was captured and sent to the provost in New York City, where he eventually died.[107] A study of muster roles of the Third Brigade of Delancey's Battalion from February 24, 1781, shows a John Degross listed as a "prisoner in prevost."[108] This may have been the real name of this soldier.

Another of the attackers, Isaac Algar, escaped, and after carrying out further robberies, he was recaptured. Onderdonk states that Isaac Algar and Nathaniel Parker also robbed Platt Carll and beat his family in Huntington.[109] Algar and Parker were later sentenced to death by hanging for this act. There are a number of petitions from both Algar and Parker from the provost to Sir Guy Carleton begging for mercy and pleading his innocence in the act. The petitions note certificates that state their official services were as Loyalists in the provincial regiments and as refugees. Other petitions state Alger was in the service for three years and was a pilot and that Parker was on the British lines for five years and spent two and a half years in the King's American Dragoons. Other petitions record fellow members of the King's American Dragoons seeking mercy for the men's lives.[110] A review of muster rolls from the King's American Dragoons from the period does not list the men in the regiment. Even after all these petitions for support, on September 10, 1783, a detachment of cavalry served as an escort for a procession that took its route through the village of Huntington and up a hill to the gallows, which, at the time, was a huge oak tree. Following the cavalry was an oxcart containing two coffins. Behind the coffins were the offenders, Isaac Algar and Nathaniel Parker, walking on foot. At the site of Gallows Hill on the eastern side of the village, the two men were hanged. The site of Gallows Hill can still be seen today at the intersection of roads near the spot marking Fort Hill in Huntington.[111]

The two men are documented as being tried on August 21, 1783, in New York and executed in New York in 1783 for the charge of "robbing a dwelling house."[112]

In April 1782 in Flushing, a party of soldiers with blackened faces attacked James Hedger and shot him to death in his bedroom. They robbed him of £200 in coin and a large amount of clothing and silverware. Colonel Hamilton offered a £150 reward for the detection of the criminals and a free pardon to any accomplices who gave evidence. The story is that a soldier named Perrot confessed that the crime was committed by him and five other members of the

A section of an early map showing Gallow's Hill. The intersection of roads can be seen just below the trees. From a map of the Harbor and Village of Huntington, North Shore of Long Island, 1837. *Courtesy of the University Libraries Digital Research Collections, Stony Brook University.*

Thirty-Eighth and Fifty-Fourth Regiments. A couple of the criminals managed to escape, but three of the men were arrested at Lloyd's Neck and brought back to Flushing, where their units had been before they were moved to Bedford. They were all tried, and two of the men were hanged from a chestnut tree in the presence of their entire brigade.[113]

It is interesting that in both of these stories of military executions, a mention is made of Provost Marshal William Cunningham being present and acting as executioner. William Cunningham's history has been passed down as that of a brutal and notorious jailor for the British army in New York City. Formerly, he was part of the Sons of Liberty movement in New York but broke from the group after getting injured in a fight near New York's Liberty Pole in 1775 and getting badly beaten. He then became a strong Tory and joined the British administration in Boston and moved with the army to New York. He is said to have caused the deaths of thousands of American prisoners during the war, selling their provisions, exchanging their goods for spoiled food and even poisoning them. Supposedly, 250 prisoners were taken out of their confinements in New York and hanged secretly without trial from gallows behind the barracks. There are other tales that tell of him hanging 5 or 6 prisoners every night in New York City.[114]

Within its own ranks, the British military had a strict system of enforcing justice. Punishments were in fact meant to terrorize those who witnessed the acts. The trials themselves were public performances, and the sentences were engineered for publicity and fear for the other soldiers. Typically, the men of the offender's regiment were assembled to hear the charge, proceedings and sentencing of the court-martial and witness the punishment in the form of either executions or floggings. The corporal punishment of flogging was to be inflicted by the drummers of the regiment in the presence of all officers and soldiers.[115]

A detail of woodcut of a British military flogging, 1853. *Wikimedia Commons.*

Lastly, the British troops themselves were subject to a type of abuse in the form of guerrilla warfare from local inhabitants sympathetic to independence. Soldiers who were sometimes separated from their forces would be found dead by the roadside. They would be ambuscaded in the woods or passageways leading to their stations. Many of these attacks took place in Huntington on the roadways connecting the village to the garrison and headquarters on Lloyd's Neck. Young Patriots would hide along the roadside within the woods at Mutton Hollow (today's Southdown Road) and pick off the British soldiers whenever they were found in small numbers.[116]

The story of a prank was recorded in which a few rebel youths set a trap along the main West Neck Road between Huntington village and Lloyd's Neck. The spot was the location of the old Alexander Sammis house, which remains today very close to the intersection of present-day School Lane. British officers would frequently ride along West Neck Road during the day and night, and the sound of galloping horses would awaken the locals from their sleep. This constant annoyance inspired a young member of the Sammis family and a neighborhood friend to stretch a rope across the road at a rise of ground a little north of the old house. The rope was set at a height so it would throw a man from his horse as he galloped past. The young men gathered their family guns and hid behind a stone wall opposite the Sammis house, waiting for the trap to be sprung. As several officers approached, the boys could hear the rhythm of the horses galloping and the chatter of the men. When the soldiers had almost reached the boys, there was suddenly an abrupt end to the noise. The officers had been thrown from their horses into the roadway. This must have been a terrible shock to the riders, who were then subjected to the loud roar of the musket shots from the boys hidden behind the wall. Frightened, the officers assumed that they were under attack. In this excitement and panic, the boys made their escape.[117]

In light of this almost humorous story, mostly all the recorded stories tell of abuses inflicted that could have and sometimes did end in death. The records tell of acts of violence and torture that are very dramatic and personal. One can only imagine that many more stories were never recorded.

5

DRAGOONS

British dragoon forces appear to have been the first troops to take over and harass local American forces and militias after the capture of Long Island in 1776. Long Island's low-lying geography allowed for the rapid movement and stationing of cavalry forces across the island. As early as August 28, 1776, the British Seventeenth Light Dragoons harassed American light horse soldiers, who had been driving cattle off to avoid their capture by the enemy. Two soldiers were captured by these dragoons as they were attempting to escape across Long Island Sound. The captured men were sent to prison in New York City.[118]

Members of the same dragoon force quickly occupied the village of Newtown on Long Island, close to the city. Leading Whigs were imprisoned or sent into exile, and their property was seized. "The light horse scoured the town and while it was yet early, guided by one George Rapelye, a loyalist, came along the Poor Bowery, and halted at Jacobus Lent's (late Isaac Rapelye's) to get some bread. Brandishing their naked swords, they declared that they were in pursuit of that damned rebel Doctor Riker."[119]

Once the forces had occupied Queens County, the troops remained encamped in the fields, and the officers were quartered in private homes in and around Newtown. Queens residents had to tip their hats to the officers outdoors and stand like inferiors when speaking to them on the streets.[120] Later, after the retreat of Washington's forces from New York City, the Seventeenth Light Dragoons took part in the Battle of White Plains and then moved to more southern theaters of war until 1778.

An illustration of a troop of the British Seventeenth Light Dragoons. *From J.W. Fortesque's* History of the 17th Lancers.

In 1778, the Seventeenth Light Dragoons wintered in Hempstead, Long Island, and made the village their headquarters. Hempstead, at the time of the war, was small, with only nine houses between the brooks surrounding it. The British selected the location as an outpost for the cavalry, as it was close enough to the city of New York to provide aid in case of attack. It also allowed the unit to make excursions into the Long Island countryside to gather forage and supplies and to also scout for attackers from the northern side of the island. American intelligence recorded, "I this day also learn that the Light Infantry from Jamaica, with the 17th Dragoons and Cathcart's Legion, from Jerico, are Order'd to South and East Hampton's and as they take no Provission with them, it is believ'd they will sweep all that Country."[121]

Records state that the Presbyterian church in Hempstead was used as a barracks for soldiers and that a chimney was added for their warmth. The building was purported to have been later converted into a guardhouse and then to a riding and drilling school for the light horse soldiers. Along the brook east of the village, soldiers' huts were built with sod. There was a woodyard and hay magazine created north of Sammis's Tavern that was closed in and guarded. Hempstead had essentially become a military camp. The British officers made an effort to keep the men under control, and two places where the men were punished were recorded. Men were picquetted near the Presbyterian church and also behind Sammis's Tavern. Floggings were also commonly held in the Presbyterian burial ground.[122] A period military document called "The Discipline of the Light Horse" describes, "Court Martials are only to be called on extraordinary occasions; and whipping used as seldom as possible: it is recommended, to endeavour to pique the men in honour to behave well, and to make them sensible of their faults, without proceeding, if possible, to extremities."[123]

The Post diary tells of a robbery in 1780 in which the attackers wore black masks and were armed with cutlasses and silvered pistols. They broke into the house of a person named Joseph Willets, who was of some age. They inquired about the location of his money, and after he offered only his timepiece, they became enraged. One of the robbers struck the old man with his cutlass, and as he stooped to avoid the blow, he was hit severely on the cheek. The diary later describes that a report of the attack was made to the captain of a company of troops quartered at Jericho. Three men of the unit were found to have been absent on the night of the attack. The men were recognized by members of the household where the attack took place. Mr. Willets personally pleaded for the guilty men to not be dealt with severely. The men, however, were dealt with severely by what they called picquetting.[124] Its more than likely that the culprits were troopers of the Seventeenth Light Dragoons.

The commanding officer of the Seventeenth Light Dragoons in Hempstead was Lieutenant Colonel Samuel Birch. Judge Thomas Jones says that in 1779, Colonel Birch sent a party to Secatogue, which was twenty miles east of Hempstead, and had them pull down a Quaker meetinghouse

An early photograph of the Sammis Tavern, located on the northeast corner of Main and Fulton Streets in Hempstead, date unknown. *Courtesy of the Hempstead Public Library.*

Northern view of Hempstead (L.I.) N.Y., (1840). *The Miriam and Ira D. Wallach Division of Art, Prints and Photographs, New York Public Library Digital Collections.*

and bring back all its materials for his own use. Upon the troops' return, they also took out all the sash windows from the house of Judge Jones at Fort Neck.[125] The same year, Birch also had the Presbyterian meetinghouse in Foster's Meadow pulled down and the materials brought away for his own use. Birch had become a dreaded personality within the town, as he confiscated buildings, houses and furniture for his own comfort.[126]

Lieutenant Colonel Birch was also the commander responsible for a grisly spectacle that was surely known throughout the countryside for some time. In the summer of 1779, three privates under his command broke into a dwelling house and, in their haste, had awakened the family. In a resulting skirmish involving the choking of the homeowner's sister, one of the soldiers was shot through the throat and killed. The other soldiers were also captured and released. Judge Jones later accused Birch of discharging the criminals without a trial. Birch, having been criticized, decided to insult the townspeople by condemning only the dead soldier and not the others. Birch told the townspeople to take notice of how the military defended them. The dead soldier was tried, condemned and sentenced to be hanged in chains.[127]

Hanging in chains, or gibbeting, was a post-mortem punishment. It was used rarely, but the spectacle had great effect. The dead body was encased in a strong iron frame. Around the neck, a heavy iron collar was placed, from which four curved iron bands rose over the head and face, meeting at the crown of the head. Above that, the body was fastened to a heavy ring. This

A Gibbet, undated. *Thomas Rowlandson, 1756–1827, British, Yale Center for British Art, Paul Mellon Collection, B1975.3.137.*

ring was strongly affixed to a crossbeam and post, which suspended the body in midair. From the neckband, the frame then extended down the body and ended in bands around the legs and below the knees.[128]

The grotesque display of the condemned had many purposes:

> *Gibbeting was intended to inspire terror among witnesses and onlookers. It involved suspending the corpse of a convicted murderer between earth and sky, thereby exiling the criminal body to a liminal space, and leaving it there for up to several decades until there was little, if anything left. For the condemned, sentencing made them aware that their body would be denied proper burial, and would be exposed, subject to public scorn, and would visibly decay, drop and be devoured by animals and insects. The criminal body might be further subjected to the ignominy of being stolen or carried off—at times, piece by piece—as decay allowed bones to fall through the gibbet cage onto the ground. In other cases, decay left an assemblage of bony body parts in the cage from which they could not easily be extracted.*[129]

It was also hoped the spectacle would inspire fear and act as a deterrent for other criminals within the ranks. It was expected that the convicted would be aware that their body would be denied the rights of proper funeral and burial and that their remains would inspire terror and revulsion to onlookers. "The humiliating display of the body, its eerie and uncanny motion on the gibbet, and the disgusting smells and excretions emanating from the corpse as it decomposed, all contributed to this spectacular, arresting punishment."[130]

In 1935, a skeleton with a skull bound tightly in an iron cage was found by a youngster named Ruddy Gorman, who was playing on the side of a

Human Head Found Locked in An Iron Cage in 1935. From Reddit, For All Things Creepy Blog.

sand pile on a vacant lot on Main Street near Union Place in Hempstead. After the remains were found, a search was made at all local and county courts to reveal any cases that would have precured a punishment of this manner. It was initially thought the remains were those of an enslaved person who had been sentenced without a trial. Another conjecture was that the body was that of a Native who was captured and condemned during early colonial wars.[131]

The most convincing record was found in Henry Onderdonk Jr.'s writings about the incident: "The body of the dead man (Silby of the 60th regiment, others say of the 17th dragoons) was hung in an iron frame on a gibbet, on the Plains north of Hempstead, and his regiment paraded before it. The creaking of the iron, as it swung to and fro by the wind, would often alarm the nightly traveller."[132]

In a review of the muster rolls of the Seveneeth Light Dragoons by this author, the individual was determined to be Private Robert Silby of Francis Needham's company of the dragoons. He is listed as a casualty from May 1780, with the notation, "Died 20 October."[133]

The site of the gibbet was instrumental to the persuasion of the audience and to the power of the enforcing entity. In the case of Robert Silby, the gibbet was located along a main route at the entry point to Hempstead Village from the plains. This site was planned, allowing both maximum visual exposure and the gathering of larger crowds to view the spectacle. It was also far enough from the village center so that its unpleasantries were not in constant view. As mentioned in Onderdonk's record, the gibbet made creaking noises that alarmed individuals. Subsequently, the design of the gibbet caused the body to sway in the wind, and the metal-on-metal sound of the hook and chain caused an eerie noise that was especially unsettling at night.[134]

Another unit that wintered on Long Island during the war and had a troop of cavalry was a Loyalist force called the Queen's Rangers, commanded by Lieutenant Colonel John Graves Simcoe. The unit frequently quartered in the village of Oyster Bay on the north shore of the island. The Queen's Rangers was a well-trained unit that arrived for winter cantonment in November 1778. After that winter, the unit was, for periods, on Long Island and usually between campaign seasons. Their uniforms were green and white, and their initial numbers in 1778 were 360 men. The rangers had both infantry and cavalry troops in the regiment, and the initial hussar (cavalry) troop was created in late 1778.[135] Like the quarters of the Seventeenth Light Dragoons in Hempstead, Oyster Bay became a safe collection point of supplies, and the dragoons of the Queen's Rangers made forage collections to the eastern and interior parts of the island. The unit was highly disciplined and took advantage of its winter quartering to further its training and battle tactics.[136] "The light infantry, and Huzzars, were put under the direction of Captain Saunders, who taught them to gallop through the woods, and acting together, the light infantry learnt to run, by holding the horse' manes; the cavalry were, also, instructed as the infantry lay flat upon the ground, to gallop through their files."[137]

Captain John Saunders (circa 1789), W. 6995. *Courtesy of the New Brunswick Museum.*

In August 1779, Simcoe also brough a company of Buck's County dragoons and a Hessian unit called Captain Diemar's Independent Company of Hussars to the Oyster Bay area. Lord Rawdon wrote to Diemar:

> *A number of Brunswick soldiers, prisoners under the convention of Saratoga, had escaped from Virginia and got into New York. There were no officers*

of their own troops to take charge of them…and it was impracticable to attach them to any Hessian regiment.…They were very disorderly. To keep them under discipline…Sir H. Clinton ordered them to be formed into a temporary corps of Hussars; such a corps being wanted at the outposts, and the nature of the service being supposed agreeable to the men.[138]

The men of the unit wore a hussar cap and black coat with blue trousers and boots of the hussar style, that is with a short boot and the trousers worn tucked in. Their jackets are assumed to have been a similar style to those of the Prussian hussars of the time. Half of the troops were armed with muskets and bayonets, and the other half were armed with carbines and carbine belts.[139] Diemar's company was also known as the Black Hussars. It was believed that Diemar's company of hussars was not stationed in the village of Oyster Bay with the Queen's Rangers but near the home of Rem Hegeman, just south of Glen Cove in the Cedar Swamp district between the east and west hillsides.[140]

The British Legion, another combined provincial cavalry and infantry unit, was also quartered on Long Island. The unit was commissioned by Lord Cathcart in 1778. Shortly after its organization, its leadership passed to Colonel Banastre Tarleton, who commanded the cavalry, and Major Charles Cochrane, who commanded the infantry. The legion, early in the war, had four infantry companies and three cavalry troops, with a combined strength of 333 men.[141]

A Light Infantry Man and Huzzar of the Queen's Rangers (circa 1780). Diemar's company of hussars historically would have been in similar dress. *Toronto Public Library Digital Archive.*

The British Legion's cavalry wintered in both 1778 and 1779 in the Jericho area, and the infantry wintered in Oyster Bay and Jericho. The troops of dragoons ravished the countryside from Jericho to Smithtown in 1778–79, collecting forage for the British army's use.

Seth Norton, a forage master for the British army in Oyster Bay, made frequent complaints about the legion's conduct. He stated, "Two or three days ago they were at Wolver Hollow about four miles from this, taking all kinds of Forage without granting receipts, the Inhabitants make frequent complaints and Col. Simcoe has once sent out a Party with Mr. Dix & drove them off." He continued, "They returned the next day and they have at Jericho, including the Plain Hay more Forage than the number of horses now they ought to consume this season."[142]

A part of the British Legion's infantry is listed as present in a muster dated February 23, 1779, from Sagg, which was a village near Southampton on the east end of the island. Records also list the British Legion being present in Sag Harbor in 1779. In an extract from a general court-martial that occurred in Southampton in March 1779, a private dragoon of the legion named Thomas Connoly was accused of highway robbery. The testimony is proof that a part of the British Legion's cavalry troops was also in the area at the time.

Daniel Sanford Inhabitant being duly sworn saith that on Tuesday the Second day of this present month, about a mile to the East of Southampton the Prisoner overtook him on the Highway on Horseback with Pistols before him and Stoped this Evidence asking him if he had got any money, he ordered him to deliver up what he had, and asked if he had no Guineas. On the Evidence answering he had not the Prisoner claped a pistol to his breast saying Damn you deliver your purse or you are a dead man, he was then afraid and gave the Prisoner his purse containing two York Shillings in Silver and fourteen Coppers (for halfpence) which purse being produced in Court the Evidence Swears it to be the identical purse of which the Prisoner robbed him, after he took his purse the Prisoner seemed very angry and Damning him said where is your watch and after Striking him several times with his naked sword and having caused him to turn out his Pockets, the Prisoner finding neither Watch nor Guineas Struck him again several times, and pointing to a house nigh he asked the Evidence if there was any money in that house the Evidence in hopes to get rid of him said there was and turning toward the house the Evidence saw the man of the House at work at the Barn shewing the Prisoner the man of the House he went with the Prisoner towards the Barn and while he was engaged with this Countryman the Evidence got off and further saith not.[143]

The outcome of the court-martial was that Thomas Connoly was found guilty of highway robbery and was to "Suffer death: that he be taken from the place of his Confinement to the place of execution & their hung by the Neck till he is dead."[144]

Thomas Connoly is listed in muster rolls as Thomas Connolly, who was part of Captain Robert Hovenden's troop of the legion's light dragoons.

Contrary to the sentencing, Connolly must have been pardoned or had his punishment revoked, as he was still listed in the rolls of the troop in both 1781 and 1782.[145]

One of the last provincial regiments raised during the war was the King's American Dragoons. This corps was proposed in 1780 as a New England cavalry unit, and its command was assigned to Benjamin Thompson. Many of its officers had served in the ranks of Governor Wentworth's Volunteers, another cavalry troop. Despite the high discipline of the corps, its uniformity and thorough training, it never served in any battle or skirmish of the war. In addition to new recruits, the corps also received drafts from such units as the Loyal New Englanders, the Volunteers of New England, Governor Wentworth's volunteers and Stewart's troop of light dragoons. The regiment was organized into six troops with attached light artillery, as not all of the men were mounted.[146] The regiment wintered in Huntington in 1782, and it became notorious, with its commander Benjamin Thompson desecrating the town's burial ground with the construction of Fort Golgotha.

6

HESSIANS

Auxiliary troops were used by the British army throughout the struggle with the American colonies. It was not unusual to use foreign troops in eighteenth-century warfare. England was, at the time, closely tied to northern Germany through the house of Hanover. The military effectiveness of the Germans made them valuable assets to the British empire. Military service was a common path for young Germans, and their employment was a readily available source of income for both them and their rulers.[147]

From 1776 to 1782, the British employed over thirty thousand German soldiers, with approximately twenty thousand troops in America at any one time and almost equaling the size of the British army. Representatives of Great Britain and Hessen-Cassel in January 1776 agreed that the Hessians would furnish twelve thousand men to serve under the British command in North America. The corps comprised a general staff, four battalions of grenadiers, fifteen battalions of infantry and two companies of "chasseurs" (jäger), the whole provided with necessary officers. Each battalion was to be provided with two pieces of field artillery and the necessary officers, gunners and other persons, along with an accompanying train.[148]

Hessian troops were used in the Battle of Long Island in 1776. After the battle, the Hessians were positioned specifically on Long Island to supplement the garrisoning and provisioning function of the troops in the occupied region.[149] The units that were stationed for periods on the island were described as a "rowdy lot amongst themselves."[150] They sometimes quarreled at evening gatherings and then settled things the next morning with duels by sword in the local fields.[151]

The Hessians spent months wintering on Long Island throughout the war. In 1778, the troops of the Hesse-Hanau Regiment Erbprinz were positioned in camps in Brooklyn, the Regiment Prinz Carl were encamped in Bushwick and troops of the Anspach and Jagers were camped in Flushing. In 1779, Von Donop's regiment was positioned at Bushwick, and the Prince of Hesse's infantry were quartered in the Newtown area. There were soldiers billeted along the Black Stump Road and in or near Ryerson's Inn, which was a famous stopping place for troops moving east and west on Long Island.[152]

The Hessians who came to America were rumored to be barbaric mercenaries, and this perspective preceded their arrival in each new area that they entered in the conflict. Wherever the Hessians went, the local inhabitants reacted with fear and alarm. They had been told tales that the Hessians were not human and that they plundered everyone and burned and killed everything in their path. Many Americans were told that the Germans ate small children.[153]

The Hessians received criticisms from not only the enemy but from their British allies as well. A British period journal records:

> *The Ravages committed by the Hessians, and all Ranks of the Army, on the poor Inhabitants of the Country, make their case deplorable; the Hessians destroy all the fruits of the Earth without regard to Loyalists or Rebels, the property of both being equaly a prey to them, in which our Troops are too ready to follow their Example, and are too much Licensed to it.*[154]

Whether the Hessians acted differently from other military units of the time is questionable. Most likely, they were being singled out because they were different and because they were foreigners. Many of the fears of the Hessians stemmed from the troops' look and attire. Their uniforms and grooming styles were different from those most accepted among the English military and domestic classes of the time in British North America.

> *The Hessian had a towering brass-fronted cap, (some had three-cornered hats,) mustachios colored with the same material that colored his shoes, (which were square toed, turned up, and had large buckles,) his hair plastered with tallow and flour, and tightly drawn into a long queue, reaching to his waist; a blue uniform, almost covered by broad belts that sustained his cartouch box, his brass hilted sword, and his bayonet; a yellow waistcoat with flaps, and yellow breeches met at the knee by black gaiters.*[155]

Hessen-Cassel: Füsilier-Regt. v. Knyphausen, 1776-83. in voller Feldausrüstung: Säbel nach englischer Art über der Brust, Feldflasche, Tornister, Brotbeutel, Zeltpflöcke und Beilpicke.

A Hessian soldier from the Fusilier Regiment von Knyphausen, 1776–83. *Property of Johannes Schwalm Historical Association Inc., in Scotland, Pennsylvania.*

The reoccurring fears and stereotypes were recorded in Newtown, Long Island, in the early years of the war: "The Hessians wore a blue dress—with varied facings—usually white —all wore black gaiters, etc.…The German army wore mustaches. Hessians wore much Hair on face—looked frightfully."[156]

Most Americans, in time, came to realize that their fears were held in folly. Those who had vacated their dwellings in fear of the coming of the Hessians later returned to their homes. Many Americans expressed disappointment upon realizing that their anxieties were unfounded, discovering that the Hessians looked and acted just like other human beings.[157]

In fact, most Hessian conscripts were not hardened, seasoned career fighters. Most were poor and most likely in debt or in trouble for some petty crime or had merely been impressed by army recruiters. Unlike the noted criticism in the British journal previously discussed, many Hessians saw their English army allies as much more barbaric. In Von Kraft's journal, he recorded acts of the British soldiery as "frightful occurrences, of theft, fraud, robbery and murder by the English soldiers, which their love of drink excited; and as they received but little money, they used these disgusting means."[158]

A large contingent of Hessian forces was stationed farther east on Long Island starting in the winter of 1780. The plundering of New England vessels from the sound had become more frequent, and strong detachments from the Connecticut mainland roamed the Long Island countryside. The French army had finally arrived to bolster the American army with a build-up of troops in the Newport, Rhode Island area. These events posed a critical threat to Long Island. Troops of the Hessian jäger corps were sent along the north shore of Long Island to aid in its defense. On November 28, 1780, the corps crossed from New York into Long Island and arrived on November 29 in the area of Westbury. Their goal was to occupy a cordon along the Long Island Sound. The left flank held Cow Bay, Cow Neck, Searingtown and Hempstead Harbors. The commanders', Wurmb's, Donop's, Hinrichs's and Prueschenck's, companies occupied the center area from Westbury to Mosquito Cove. Lieutenant Colonel Wurmb was quartered in Westbury. To the east, two Anspach jäger companies, under the command of Captain Waldenfels, were billeted at Jericho. At Oyster Bay, the Queen's Rangers were on the right flank, and the mounted jägers were stationed at Norwich. The entire line was over two miles long, with about one thousand men in total.[159]

The forces quartered in mostly single-family houses, in which ten to twelve troops were grouped together in one spot. The positioning of the entire corps was a cantonment, with the main roads to any of the bays and landings of the sound occupied by pickets of each company. The pickets required straw huts to be built for the winter, and large fires needed to be maintained for warmth. At the lieutenant colonels' quarters at the center, a redoubt was built on a height. It was stationed with a guard and two cannons.[160]

Onderdonk reported that on Long Island, the Hessians might have made a better impression than the British: "The Hessians were more sociable than the English soldiers, and often made little baskets and other toys for the children, taught them German and amused them in various ways; sometimes corrupting them by their vile language and manners."[161]

Lydia Post, in the Post diary, recorded of the Hessians, "The soldiers take so much notice of the children, that I fear lest they should contact evil, especially Charles. They have taught him to speak their language; he understands nearly all their conversation. They make pretty little willow baskets for Marcia and Grace, and tell them of their own little ones at home, over the stormy ocean."[162]

In November 1783, in a correspondence between Sir Guy Carleton to the landgrave of Hesse Cassel, General de Lossberg and Carleton confirmed the professional merits of the Hessian forces: "Lieutenant General de Lossberg being on the point of sailing on his return to Europe, testifies to his merit and good conduct and the exemplary behaviour of the Hessian troops under his orders during the time he (Carleton) has had the honour of commanding this army."[163]

For the most part, the Hessians held a high impression of Long Island.

> Long Island is a beautiful island. It has a multitude of meadows, tilled fields, fruit trees of all kinds, and fine houses.
>
> The section around Jamaica is very charming and mostly level. From there a road runs to Hemstead, where there are fine plains with hills running along the side and small woods. Hemstead is a church-town with two churches, one English and one Presbyterian; it has extensive territory, although very few houses stand in Hemstead proper. The inhabitants, as upon the whole island, are rich, well-to-do people, who have the real wealth of the state; i.e., they are rich landowners. There are many Quakers here.
>
> The whole island is like a painted landscape. You can hardly go an English mile in these two counties [King's and Queen's Counties] without finding houses. The inhabitants are lively, and usually rascals at heart. The air here is still (in September) very pleasant. Winter begins with December and lasts till the beginning or end of March.[164]

"List of British Soldiers Quartered at Jericho, 1783." *From Hofstra University's Long Island Studies Institute, Nassau County Museum Reference Collection.*

The Hessians may have held a high impression of the land itself, but this may not have been true of their feelings for the war and their American opponents. At least in this one account, Private Jung Heim wrote to his parents of his feelings about the American soldiery:

> *About the American war here I can't write much except it is a bad war. The soldiers we oppose, the American farmers, are no regular soldiers. They are more like robbers and thieves in that they hide in hedges and bushes and shoot so well, when they are able, that they hit every time. They also wear their farmers' clothes. I can't write you anything good about them.* [165]

The Hessian forces also frequently dealt with the problem of troop desertion. In 1778, the Hessian command tried to use executions as a deterrent for troops leaving the ranks. Some soldiers were executed as a result. Enlisted Hessian subjects were not legally allowed to be released from their enlistments. Still, some of the troops of the Hessian forces, such as those of Kassel, were suggested by command to the authorities that they be allowed to stay in America if they so desired.[166] It was apparent that by the Battle of Yorktown in 1781, the war was winding down. It seems that some German troops and even new recruits had become aware of opportunities in America and were planning to stay in the colonies.

Orders from Hessian command in 1781 stated:

> *Free pardon to all non-commissioned officers and privates, deserters from the Hessian Corps.*
>
> *LOSSBERGH, Commander-in-Chief Of the Auxiliary Troops of Hesse.* [167]

In a report from Lieutenant Colonel Wurmb in Jericho in 1781, he recorded that many more families were accompanying the new enlistments, possibly for immigration to America.

> *The Corps is fairly well; but we have too many unusable people who arrive with every recruit transport. Some old and wholly unusable people, from Kassel of all places. I can only believe that the family must bribe Captain Romstatt to enlist them. I further must request that Captain Romstatt not to enlist so many married men and to take on men with*

whole families last. The Corps has more wives and children than men. This causes much complaint in the Corps.[168]

Many of the German men were trained in crafts for which there was a need in American communities, and many came from rural backgrounds, giving them a particular appreciation for the land. Several Hessians chose to stay in America and on Long Island to begin new lives when the war ended.

7

RAIDERS

R aids by Americans from Connecticut to disrupt the British wartime efforts on Long Island escalated as the war progressed. Many of the Patriot refugees who left Long Island early in the war were involved in these raids. This struggle across the sound became much more of a civil war, at times involving local townsmen from differing sides who took refuge or remained on Long Island. Initially, Americans acted under commissions from the governors of New York and Connecticut to cruise in the sound against British vessels. They used whaleboats as their means of transportation, and parties from Connecticut started raids on Long Island shortly after the Battle of Long Island.[169]

Initially, raids were planned as a means to rescue property left behind by refugees who had left the island and to punish and harass local Tories and British forces. By 1781, this whaleboat warfare had degenerated into a rash of raids, apparently due to a proclamation by Governor Trumbull of Connecticut, which could almost be interpreted as encouraging attacks on all residents of Long Island, indiscriminate of which side they were on. Connecticut juries viewed all inhabitants of Long Island as loyal subjects of King George III and legitimate targets to thus be deprived of their property.[170] The raiders, subsequently, in their ongoing raids, were increasingly charged as plunderers more intent on robbery than on harassing the enemy.

Stories in the Lydia Post diary record a number of assaults on inhabitants of Long Island:

Illustration of Cowboys and Skinners Plundering Civilians. From Fenimore Cooper's The Spy, *1821.*

> *But worse than all, robbers come over from the main shore in boats, and keep us in constant alarm! They belong to no party, and spare none; freebooters, cowardly midnight assassins, incendiaries, indiscriminate, bold, and daring. Their hand is against every man, and every man's hand is against them.*[171]

Another account records:

> *A tale of horror has just come to our ears; we have not heard the details, nor do I wish to, they are so horrible. It seems the Runners entered the house of John Wilson, and threatened, until the wife, to save the life of her husband, revealed the hiding place. But it was too late; he died the next morning from a sabre-cut which he then received, cleaving the skull and occasioning so great loss of blood. The villains took a large sum of money, which was in silver coin, in bags under the hearthstone. Mr. Wilson was much beloved in the neighborhood; his death produced the greatest excitement and indignation.*[172]

Lieutenant Caleb Brewster wrote in 1781 to Governor Clinton from Fairfield, Connecticut, about attacks in the village of Miller's Place. He recorded that around midnight on August 14, two boats landed at Miller's Place. The crew of one of the boats demanded entrance at the house of Captain Ebenezer Miller, asking for his arms, which he freely gave up. His son, on opening an upper window while trying to determine the alarm, was shot dead. The other crew visited the home of Andrew Miller, and when he opened the door for them, he was struck on the head with the breech of a gun, which broke the bone over his eye, damaging his eye and breaking his cheek bone.[173]

Many of the Long Island inhabitants fought back against the raiders, the Lydia Post diary records:

> The robbers have been over already; they landed last night at the harbor. In the dead of night they surrounded the house of John Pearsall. He is called rich, and there is no doubt they counted on large booty. Their first care is generally to prevent escapes, lest the alarm should be given to the neighbors. Whenever they have reason to think that any one has escaped to inform, they invariably scamper fearing surprise. On finding his house so hemmed in, Mr. Pearsall, who was the only man in the house, made a great noise and blustering, calling Tom, John, and Harry to load and fire, then ran to the top of the house with the gun, and fired three times in quick succession. The robbers took the alarm, jumped into the boat, and shoved off.[174]

In Miller's Place, at the same home of the attack of Andrew Miller noted previously, a story says that Timothy Miller added two heavy iron bars set in sockets of wood on either side of the door to reinforce the heavy two-handled (Dutch) front door that had only a wooden lock. He also planned that if the front door should give way to attack, he would defend his tiny front hall by firing at close range from three loopholes he cut into the door in his west room.[175]

Today, the front hall that Timothy Miller meant to defend still exists in its eighteenth-century state in the surviving William Miller house. The sockets of wood on either side of the front door still exist, and the wooden bars seen today could have been actual metal bars at the time. There are still three holes cut above the door to the west room, but these holes have since been proven to not be from the Revolutionary period. Also, the angle of fire toward the front door does not seem plausible. There could have been former loopholes in the face of this door that could have been later repaired, and/or the door could have been replaced.

The Miller family of Miller's Place was a family divided along partisan lines. Captain Ebenezer Miller, whose son was shot in the upstairs window, was a strong Patriot and a militia officer. His brother Timothy Miller of the same village refused to sign on as an associator in 1775. Richard Miller, a cousin of the Millers, also refused to sign. Richard was an ardent Tory and recruited for the British army. He became so unpopular in the area that he had to go into hiding. He was killed by a Patriot force from the mainland in Selden in 1776.[176]

The existing front hall at the William Miller House. This image shows the wooden bars and supports at the front door and the debated possible loopholes above the door in the background. Miller Place. *Photograph by author.*

As the war progressed, authorities on the mainland began to tighten restrictions on Connecticut citizens who were also possibly going to Long Island to take part in the trafficking of illegal goods. Illicit trafficking was the trade of imported goods, particularly of those from England. Since the beginning of the war, it was illegal for the English to trade with rebellious American subjects. With the English trade influx halted during the war and the mainland having been deprived of the many English luxuries of the day, many began to once again desire these goods. The demand for tea, silks and other European items rose greatly, and with it came the beginnings of the illicit trade. Sometimes by arrangement, a storekeeper on Long Island would stock up on forbidden items of this illicit trade and arrange for a friendly captain from Connecticut to stage a raid with a whaleboat party to acquire the items. The items, in this case, would have been paid for beforehand at a private conference. After the items were sold on the mainland, the money was divided up among the raiders. Those in the illicit trade were able to benefit greatly from these business efforts.[177]

Meanwhile, as some of the refugees from Connecticut came back to procure supplies, they were liable to be robbed by those same raiders from Connecticut. Ebenezer Dayton, a refugee from Long Island, was called the "head of the banditti," and he made frequent excursions from Connecticut to raid the island.[178]

The story of a Quaker who showed extreme neighborliness to his attackers and thus survived the ordeal unscathed is recorded in the Post diary.

> *The Runners came over from the main shore to attack the house of Stephen Willets, a Quaker; he stands high in the Society as a preacher, and devout man. The family had retired; he first took the alarm, and knew in a moment that his time of trial had come. When the attackers approached he threw open the door and said, "Walk in friends and warm yourselves, it is chilly this evening." He Threw wood on the fire, and kept talking so kindly, that the men, though ever so evilly disposed, had not time to say a word. He then went and called at the foot of the stairs for his servant; "Caesar, come down; get ready some supper for these friends. They must be very cold, and need refreshment." Minced pies, meat and bread. Were put upon the table, and cider ordered to be drawn. The robbers looked at each other in silent amazement; but the old man's kindness was so pressing, and seemed so hearty, it was out of their power to refuse; so they sat down and partook of his good cheer. After they had eaten, Mr. Willets told them when their wished their beds were ready.*

Drumming Out a Tory—A Revolutionary War Incident, by C.S. Rienhardt. *From* Harper's Weekly, *February 3, 1877.*

They were now completely overcome; their hard hearts melted, making them as unable to begin the work of plunder as though bound in chains of iron![179]

Whaleboat troops also began to carry off distinguished Loyalists in exchange for Whig prisoners. Judge Thomas Jones, already mentioned, had just been paroled after being taken prisoner again in November 1779 and robbed of £300 by a Captain David Hawley of Connecticut. Hawley and his men landed at Stonybrook on the north shore of Long Island and marched fifty-two miles to Fort Neck and surprised and captured Jones. The captain had been seeking someone suitable to exchange for Jones on the American side. An old classmate of Jones's, Gold Selleck Silliman, who had been captured by Loyalists from his home in Connecticut, was selected for the exchange. Jones, while in captivity, had remained at Silliman's house for a while and then was moved to Middletown. He was exchanged for Silliman in May 1780.[180]

During Judge Jones's first imprisonment in Connecticut, rebels seized four head of his cattle on Long Island. The British recaptured the cattle, which were worth £440. Jones repeatedly applied for compensation from the British but was denied. Jones was convinced that the British officials had pocketed the money. Also during Jones's second imprisonment in Connecticut, rebels again plundered his property on Long Island. A man named Chichester, who was a neighbor of Jones, guided the marauders and was later captured while trying to escape and was put in prison. Afterward, Chichester was released with no punishment whatsoever.[181]

Similarly, another Loyalist officer of the Suffolk County militia named Major Frederick Hudson, Esq., of Wading River was taken prisoner and later returned to his property. After his return home, he was plundered and robbed many times by raiders from Connecticut. Frederick Hudson, in 1775, was listed as a signer of the Brookhaven Associators of the Second Company and listed as a member of Captain Josiah Lupton's Company of Suffolk County militia in 1775.[182]

By March 1777, Hudson was reported as having recruited Loyalist troops from the east end of Long Island. It is not known what changed the political persuasion of Hudson. A letter from Captain John Davis of the Fourth New York Regiment conveys intelligence from Nathaniel Conkling, a lieutenant in the company and also refugee of Long Island: "That one Frederick Hudson a Captn of a Tory Company on Long Island had lately brought a very large quantity of Goods from New York and also one Henry Herrick of Southampton."[183]

In December 1777, Frederick Hudson was taken prisoner again by a detachment of Parson's Brigade and carried to New England. Members of the Suffolk County militia wrote to Sir Henry Clinton in March 1778, asking for assistance in his release:

> *Being very sensible of his unhappy Situation, & the Distressed feelings of his Family, as also the Wasting Condition of his Intrest, And that the whole of these Calamities are come upon him for his Loyalty and his Forwardness & Assiduity in Governments Service which Considerations Induce us humbly to pray your Excellency to think of his unhappy Situation, and if possible you can, Constantly, Direct some mthod whereby he may be restored to his Family, his Friends, & this County.[184]*

At some point between 1778 and early 1779, Frederick Hudson was released back home to Long Island and attacked.

> *A party of Rebels with their face blacked, entered the house of Fred. Hudson, Esq., of Suffolk Co., on Friday night, 6th inst., and robbed him of provisions, clothing and bedding to the amount of 200 pounds and upwards, scarcely leaving the family their wearing apparel. This is the fourth time Mr. H has been plundered since his captivity.[185]*

With the severity of the raids and to prevent robberies, a patrol was kept by the local militia along the Long Island Sound.

The militia from Wolverhollow were required to patrol on the Sound and east side of Hempstead Harbor. One night the patrol there heard the whale boats rowing, then Tunis Bogart fired, and two boats put about instantly. As they neared Cow Neck shore, E. Hegeman, a patrol on that side, also fired. One of the crew jumped up, flapped his arms, and crowed out in defiance. They then returned to the Main without affecting their design, which was to rob a store at Herricks.[186]

In Henry Onderdonk's *Incidents*, he also mentioned that there was a mounted Hessian patrol. This patrol would have been made of the men of Captain Diemar's company of hussars.

Noted as well in the Lydia Post diary was a horse guard created to defend against the attacks from the Long Island Sound. She wrote, "A company of young men is to be associated, to ride about on horseback all night; twelve go out at once, and are relieved at a certain hour by others. They are well armed, and will give the alarm where they discover signs of an intended attack."[187]

Raids from the mainland became so intolerable that certain defensive structures were erected, such as one along the Jericho Turnpike. Onderdonk wrote:

The house of James Pool, and a store kept in one of his outbuildings, were visited by a party from the Main, headed by Wright Craft. They left their borrowed horses with a sentry at the pond northwest of his house, which they loaded with booty, and returned in safety. Hoyt, to prevent similar visits, built a blockhouse, bullet proof (since removed to Herricks) with port holes in the second story, in which he kept store.[188]

In the historical will of Prince Hawes of Hempstead from October 1782, he recorded:

This is the last will and Testament of Prince Hawes, formerly of Redding, in the County of Fairfield, Colony of Connecticut but now of the township of Hempstead, Queens County, store-keeper....Whereas I own a certain Block House, which I now occupy as a store, situate near the public house or tavern of James Poole, lying upon the Great Road, north side of

A photograph of a colonial period blockhouse with loopholes overhanging the second story for defense. Fort Western, Maine. *Photograph by author.*

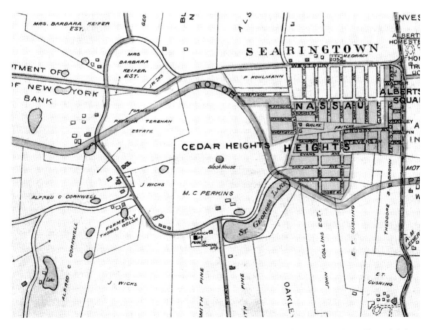

The blockhouse's location is shown just below the label for Cedar Heights. *From* A Map of Great Neck Ests-Manhasset-Roslyn-Mincola, Etc., *by Hyde, E. Belcher, 1914; New York Public Library Digital Collections.*

Hempstead Plains, I require the same to be sold at the discretion of my executors for ready money.[189]

Further research shows that Prince Hawes was actually a Loyalist from Connecticut who had fled the colony in 1776. He is listed as a member of the Reading Loyalist Association, recorded and listed in *Rivington's Gazetteer* in February 1776.[190] It is certain that he was targeted by his former townsmen from Connecticut in his attack. His efforts in fortifying his store make it apparent that he was continuously threatened for his beliefs.

Within the book *History of Queens County*, by W.W. Munsell & Co., the old blockhouse still existed at the time in the village of Herricks. It mentions that it was originally erected as a store on the Jericho Turnpike near Westbury during the American Revolution.[191] On a historical topographical map of Kings and Queens Counties, New York, dated 1854, the "Old Blockhouse" is noted just west of Herrick's Pond. There seems to be no further information about the history of the building after that time.

8

QUAKERS

Quakers, also known as members of the Religious Society of Friends, were part of a Protestant religious movement that had predominately settled in the northeastern American colonies. The Quakers on Long Island were concentrated most heavily in the western end in Queens County and at the eastern end of Suffolk County. Their settlements were some of the oldest communities on the island and included such towns as Flushing, Westbury, Bethpage, Jericho, Jerusalem and Oyster Bay. In most of these communities, they established meetinghouses.

The Society of Friends opposed the efforts of the Americans to gain independence by waging war. Their opposition was based on their religious beliefs, which rejected war and its methods. Most Quakers also had their own personal objections to taking part in the war. They believed in loyalty to a legitimate government and living in peace under the rightful ruler of the land. Thus, the Quakers swung from being politically neutral to a stance that was, at times, close to loyalism. The Quakers, however, did not actively support the British war effort.[192] This acceptance of the powers that be sometimes caused others to confuse the Quakers for outright Loyalists.

An English officer commenting on a Quaker woman's assumed beliefs said, "The members of your Society are generally supposed to be on the side of the Mother Country." She replied, "It is true they are called Tories, but unjustly, as they espouse neither cause. From their great principle, 'Resist not evil, and submission to the powers that be, they are opposed to the rising of the people against the Mother Country.'"[193]

Quakers Meeting (1809), designed and etched by Thomas Rowlandson. *The Elisha Whittelsey Collection, Metropolitan Museum of Art.*

During the Revolution, the British army occupied the majority of the Friends' meetinghouses and used them as hospitals, prisons and weapons storage facilities. The Flushing meetinghouse on Long Island was used consistently by the British army as a storage space from the Battle of Long Island in 1776 to the war's end. In the absence of their meetinghouses, the Quakers continued to worship in the homes of other Quakers.[194]

Despite the hardships placed on the Friends by the British occupiers, they remained adherent to their nonviolence testimony, using peaceful means, such as petitions, et cetera, to settle disputes. Direct assistance to the military, British or American, was always to be considered an offense.[195] As the reality of the continued British occupation set into the minds of the Quakers, the New York Meeting for Sufferings set out to establish a resolution that determined a violation of the society's peace testimony. The letter stated explicitly what was a violation, such as bearing arms, partaking in military services, dealing in prized goods, partaking in lotteries and being involved in corrupt conversations. Military service included carting supplies for the army and caring for British military horses.[196]

Some of the greatest hardships endured by the Quakers during the American Revolution were the distraints set by the militaries from both sides for not complying with military requests and orders.

Henry Post of Westbury recalled the request for him to serve in the local militia in 1774 by those supporting independence. He refused to serve and was fined. "Then came Nehemiah Sammis to my house and Demandes of me five shillings for not Appearing at a General Training and Upon my refusing to pay it he Took a Tablecloth worth 18 shillings. Henry Post. Minutes of Westbury Monthly Meeting 1774."[197]

Members of the Westbury Monthly Meeting refused to pay fines issued to them from the British army for not complying with their military orders and requests. They refused to serve on watch or stand guard as requested and would not appear to arms during periods of alarm. They would not work on various military projects that were underway, nor would they show up for military trainings. They refused to pay taxes that supported the military guard, paid for military horses or aided in the carting of goods for the military.[198]

A photograph of the Flushing Quaker Meeting House along Northern Boulevard. *Photograph by author.*

Henry Post, for the second time, was requested to serve the military, this time for the British in 1778. He recorded, "Took from me 17 shillings and 4 pence for not appearing to stand guard. Again, took 1 pound, 9s & 4p. On ye 16th of 1st mo. Daniel Toffee & Obediah Valentine, Sergeants Under Captain Cornell Demanded 5 pounds 5 s in Order to pay Some charges in building the Fort at Brooklyn & Pay the Guard as they say I Being from home they found Money and took 4 pounds 5 s. Henry Post."[199]

By April 1778, a new militia law had been passed, exempting from military service all males between the ages of sixteen and fifty-five "who in judgement of the law are or shall be of the people called Quaker." In return for this exemption, Quakers were to pay a fine of ten pounds annually when the militia was called into service. If these fines were not paid, the Quakers could be put in prison.[200]

The Quakers also refused to accept money for rent from British authorities for the use of their meetinghouses.[201]

Lydia Post's diary expresses the continued hardships of the Quakers during the occupation years: "The farmers suffer dreadfully from the levying, taxing and quartering upon them of the Hessians and British soldiers. They are very insolent, making most unreasonable demands, and the meek-spirited, unresisting Quakers are martyrs to their lawlessness and rapacity."[202]

Thomas Willis recorded another incident in which a Quaker resisted involvement with military punishment:

> *Joseph Willets, of Westbury, was robbed of 30 or 40 pounds, by some soldiers, who lay at Jericho. They maltreated him with a view of extorting more money, till his sister Sarah rushed in to avert the blows from her brother, saying, you will not strike an unarmed woman. On his making complaint to the authorities, the soldiers were drawn up in two rows, and he was ordered to walk between and point out the robbers, but the conscientious and humane Quaker relented and told the officers he could not identify them with sufficient accuracy to have them punished. So they were let off.[203]*

The unresisting and pacifist character of the Quakers caused them to suffer greatly, but in odd cases, the resolve of their character allowed them neutrality and aided in their movement between different locations in the region. For the Quakers, attending the yearly meetings and making religious visits across the military lines of both armies was frequently necessary. The Friends were granted the privilege of moving freely.

Elias Hicks, the famous preacher of Jericho, suffered with the billeting of British military authorities in his own home and at times was subjected to fines and confiscations for his refusal to aid with the building of military fortifications. Amid this, he was able to attend meetings in other areas of New York. He recorded:

> *This was a favor which the parties would not grant to their best friends, who were of warlike disposition; which shows what great advantages would redound to mankind were they all of this pacific spirit. I passed myself through the lines of both armies six times during the war without molestation, both parties generally receiving me with openness and civility; and although I had to pass over a tract of country, between the two armies, sometimes more than thirty miles in extent, and which was much frequented by robbers, a set, in general, of cruel, unprincipled banditti, issuing out from both parties, yet, excepting once, I met with no interruption even from them. But although Friends in general experienced many favors and deliverances, yet those scenes of war and confusion occasioned many trials and provings in various ways to the faithful.*[204]

Because the British government sent a fully equipped army to America that was funded by the imperial treasury, there were no military conscriptions required, nor were war taxes levied in the areas controlled by the British. Thus, Friends on the British side of the lines fared better than their brethren governed by the American authorities. This difference could be discerned in a discussion Elias Hicks had on one of his travels to American-held territory in Saratoga. He spoke with an innkeeper's wife at one of his stops, and she discovered that Hicks and his companion were from Long Island. Her being loyal to the king, she wondered why he would leave that security to come out among the Americans. Hicks informed her that as they took no part in the controversy

Elias Hicks from Bust, by William Ordway Partridge. *From* The Life and Labors of Elias Hicks, *by Henry W. Wilbur, 1910.*

and were friends to all and were principled against all wars and fighting, the contending parties all had confidence in them and let them pass freely.[205]

Other stories tell of Quakers who were not able to stand firm in their peaceful resolve. Under the constant abuse and stress of the British occupation and fear of mainland raids, some Quakers fought back. One Quaker, in the heat of passion, drew his knife against an official who was about to take his horse into military service. Another Friend decided that he would drive his wagon for the army instead of having it confiscated from him.[206] Apparently, this temporary service as a teamster was accepted by the Friends, since refusal would likely have led to the requisitioning of further supplies from the Quaker.[207] Another Quaker, overcome by the lawlessness of the time, joined a captain of the military to pursue a robber. Another, overcome by greed, purchased prized goods to be sold. In most cases, these individuals repented their actions. Some individuals, however, overcome with frustration, could not come to repent and were then disowned by the society.[208]

9

REFUGEES

The divided loyalties of inhabitants on Long Island leading up to the Revolutionary War caused tensions between both sides that continued throughout the war. Fearing for their safety and security, families had to choose the degree to which they could tolerate either the British being in authority on the island or then the Americans.

The first war refugees on Long Island came after the British defeated the Americans at the Battle of Long Island. Many inhabitants who supported independence and feared for their safety chose to leave Long Island. They naturally turned to the nearest point of the mainland, the colony of Connecticut. Even before the Battle of Long Island, the Committee of Southold had anticipated the outcome and sent its cannon and ammunition to Saybrook in Connecticut to ensure its safety.[209] Two days after the battle, the convention recommended for the inhabitants of Long Island to remove as many of their women, children, enslaved laborers, livestock and grain to the mainland as they could. The convention was to cover the expenses for the transportation.[210] Within months, large numbers of Patriot refugees crossed into Connecticut, including most of the Long Island militia. The crossings included 129 ships, many commanded by Long Island refugees.[211] Supposedly, in Sag Harbor, the boats passed for days and repassed to the Connecticut shore, freighted with Long Island inhabitants. All had abandoned their homes with nothing but the clothes they wore, some with only what they could carry.[212]

View of the Narrows between Long Island & Staaten Island with our Fleet at Anchor & Lord Howe Coming In, 12ʰ July 1776. From Archibald Robertson: His Diaries and Sketches in America, 1762–1780, *New York Public Library Digital Collections.*

On September 15, 1776, Governor Trumbull wrote to Colonel Henry Livingston, stating that "he had left to the judgement of Col. Oliver Wolcott the direction of proper means to bring the People and Stock from Long Island." Evidently, Wolcott acted quickly, for in the same month, Colonel Livingston made a raid into Suffolk County and took off 3,129 sheep and 400 head of horned cattle.[213]

Records of the State of New York also record Ezra L'Hommedieu of Southold paying for the use of ships for the transporting of goods to Connecticut: "Guildford Oct. 10. 1776—Received of Ezra L'Hommedieu Esq. nine Dollars in full for the Charter of my sloop of Twenty tons or thereabouts for transporting her Hold full of Grain & other effects from Southold on Long Island to Guildford in Connecticut."[214]

By February 1777, the governor and council of Connecticut resolved to suspend for six weeks all restraining laws in order to authorize the civil authorities and selectmen of the towns to allow and license boats for the bringing over of refugees.[215]

For the refugees, the hardships had to have been unimaginable. Their incomes were cut off, and they had a small chance of earning a living in a land in which they were refugees. The story of Captain Paul Reeve of Aquebogue tells how he had served with Colonel Josiah Smith's regiment and had to flee with his wife and five children to Saybrook, Connecticut. He took as many possessions as he could, including one yoke of oxen, eight cows, one two-year-old steer, one horse and eighteen sheep. Not long after his flight, he had to petition the governor of Connecticut to allow him to return to his Long Island estate to get more of his possessions. While he was away in refuge, his horse and six of his cows died, and he had to sell the oxen to support his family. His petition for returning was refused, but he was given a job conveying refugees from Saybrook to Dutchess County, New York.[216]

Those Patriots who chose to stay on Long Island and behind the British lines required strong moral courage. Some inhabitants had to stay to protect their aged parents or to secure their homes, as they were their only worldly belongings. Most had to remain after their friends had already left, where there were no church services and where there was no longer any sense of community. They had to live under the threat of punishment from the occupying soldiers.[217]

Reverend Joshua Hartt, the Presbyterian minister in Smithtown and an outspoken critic of the British, overtly spoke out about resistance to the British in his sermons. He refused to leave his church or stop his support for the rebels. One time when he was preaching, he was shot at, the bullet lodging in the wall above his head.[218] He was later arrested by the British and taken prisoner in 1777. He was carried in chains to the Provost Jail in New York City, where he remained for six months before being released sick with prison fever.[219]

On the opposite side, many Loyalists from other neighboring colonies had to take refuge on Long Island for their own safety. Loyalist troops were easily recruited for the British army on Long Island from the great number of loyal citizens residing there. After the war, they were forced to either leave Long Island forever or become assimilated into the new nation.

Many Loyalist refugees relocated very close to the British/Loyalist headquarters on Lloyd's Neck. It was to become the largest refugee camp of the Revolutionary War. There, the refugees lived under the pretense of semi-security from the nearby troops. The British forces did not provide food for these refugees, but they were able to provide for their families by farming and cutting wood and aiding in the British supply efforts for New York City. It is estimated that the camp reached a population of eight hundred men, with five hundred of them being armed.[220] The camps would have housed entire Loyalist families, who would have struggled to find shelter and sustenance.

Encampment of the Loyalists at Johnstown on the Banks of the River St. Lawrence in Canada, Taken June 6, 1784, by James Peachey. *Library and Archives of Canada.*

A photograph of two child-sized shoe buckles and a thimble that would fit a small child that were found at British/Loyalist troop encampment sites on Lloyd's Neck. *Artifacts from the collection of the author; photograph by the author.*

Recently, there have been many child-sized artifacts found in the remains of these refugee encampment sites on Lloyd's Neck.

The conditions in the camp were recorded by B. Birdsall in 1782 in a letter to Clinton, "I effected a four weeks' disagreeable journey—was sixteen days on the Island, during seven of which I was in camp on Lloyd's Neck. The fare in the camp is hard. It is the wickedest place I ever met with. There was no restraint, I noticed everything. The large farmers and traders do well, others are worn out."[221]

Fort Franklin was established there, and the Loyalist and refugee encampments were subject to repeated attacks and pillaging during the war, with prisoners sometimes being carried off. As the war progressed, even the southern inward shore along Lloyd Neck Harbor was subject to a constant threat of attack and robbery from the rebellious inhabitants of mainland Huntington.[222]

Seth Seely from Stamford, Connecticut, had signed a local Loyalist statement and circulated a local petition in his community of Stamford before he was deemed a Loyalist. For this, he was punished and was carried through the streets on a rail, then put in the stocks, smeared with eggs and robbed. He then went to Long Island and worked for the British as a wagoner and a woodcutter. After this, he returned to Stamford, as his wife had given birth to twins. While he was back in Stamford, he was charged and found guilty of supporting and participating in the British cause and was imprisoned in Fairfield. His property was confiscated. Seely then returned to Long Island with his family, and they all became Loyalist refugees.[223]

John Lyon of Redding, Connecticut, had a similar story. Lyon was a Loyalist who signed a resolution that protested against the establishment of the Continental Congress in his community. In 1776, he had to flee his home and join the British forces on Long Island. In 1779, he was enlisted within the Loyalist unit the Prince of Wales's American Volunteers and became a captain. Later, John Lyon and his wife, Hepzibeth, encamped as refugees at Lloyd's Neck.[224]

Long Island–born Israel Youngs of Cold Spring Harbor became a captain of a troop of horse of the Queens County militia in 1777. His unit was active in collecting forage and was called in with the local militia for the protection of the island's inhabitants from whaleboat raiders from the mainland. At some point, he relocated to New Jersey, as he was so disliked locally. It seemed he still owned property in Cold Spring Harbor. In August 1783, he was treated cruelly in an attack, and robbers carried off 1,100 of his guineas.[225] Records indicate he was robbed at three different times and was so financially ruined and destitute that it prevented him from going with other Loyalist refugees to Canada in 1783.

At the close of the war and with articles of peace being set, parts of Long Island were still trapped in a civil war, as the British military was moved to the western end of Long Island. Riots, robbery and disorderly behavior had risen in the Huntington area. The robberies and attacks on Loyalists, such as Israel Youngs, may have been a part of the noted violence. William Stephens Smith wrote to George Washington in September 1783 amid the turmoil:

In the course of the last week the riots about Huntington had rose to such a considerable Height, that Sir Guy Carleton detach'd from the Camp a regt of Cavalry and a few flank Companies to suppress it—several Persons are taken up and confined, and are said to be on their way here for trial by Court-Martial—I have my doubts—but perhaps the Circumstances of the Case may justify Sir Guy in marching his Troops in a hostile Manner into a Country from whence he had retired in consequence of the preliminary Articles of a Peace—but I am confident he might be saved that trouble in future by small parties of our Troops, possessing the Country as it becomes necessary for the British to withdraw—The Inhabitants would by adoption of this mode not only be protected from being plundered by Stragglers from the British Camp, but be Shelter'd from the rage of party Zeal, which at present threatens to blaze with an alarming Fury.[226]

Smith wrote again to Washington in October:

The detachment made from the British Camp mentioned in my last to Your Excellency for the purpose of suppressing certain riots and dis-orders near Huntington on Long Island, returned on the morning of the 29th Ulto, they have taken up a Number of the most respectable Inhabitants of that part of the Country—who are charged with robbery—confin'd in the Provost, and under tryal by General court martial, to which for near three weeks past they have been daily paraded thro' the streets in Irons.[227]

These were troubling times for all sides. Fyler Diblee from Stamford, Connecticut, formerly an attorney, was a Loyalist who fled to Long Island and served the British army. He was captured in 1778 by other Loyalists, and his property in Stamford was confiscated. His home on Long Island in the West Hills was plundered in 1779 and 1780. He was finally freed by the rebels and returned to Long Island. By 1783, he, like many others, realized

Tory Refugees on the Way to Canada (1901), by Howard Pyle. *Wikimedia Commons.*

his side had lost. Fyler Diblee sadly went to Saint John, New Brunswick, with his wife and six children and two servants but died by suicide in 1784, most likely caused by the anguish of his circumstances and ongoing struggles.[228]

Seth Seeley and John Lyon also became refugees, moving to Nova Scotia, Canada, in 1783. Diblee, Seeley and Lyon were among the six thousand Long Islanders who sailed away from Huntington Harbor at the end of the war, leaving their homeland forever. The majority of Loyalists on Long Island, however, did not leave. Most remained on the land of their birth, waiting to see how they would be treated by their victorious rebel neighbors.[229]

EPILOGUE

T he Revolutionary War on Long Island was a time of great struggle for its inhabitants. The experiences of the British occupation were memories that many hoped to forget. For Long Islanders, the end of the war was not to be the end of their suffering. Queens County still had an overwhelmingly Loyalist population. Eventually, the Loyalist population assimilated into the new nation, but punitive measures were instituted by the new government on Long Island, causing more than just the Loyalists to suffer.

With the Disenfranchisement Act established in 1784, Long Island's remaining Loyalists lost their right to vote. The number of citizens affected, estimated to be 90 percent of the population, hints at the size of the wartime loyal faction on the island.[230] The punishment of this act was not lifted until 1790. Following this, in May 1784, the State of New York also passed an act laying a tax of $37,000 on the counties of Long Island. The Patriots in the legislature looked at the fact that in Kings and Queens Counties, the enemy had found lodgment, comfort and supply.[231] The fine was also intended to compensate other parts of the state, as Long Island had not been in the condition to take a more active part against the enemy during the war. This was very unfortunate for Long Islanders, as they in fact suffered greatly and could not help that they were occupied so early on in the conflict by the enemy.

An interesting discovery made while researching the British occupation of Long Island is how much the British army and even the mainland Patriots knew the political persuasions of the island's inhabitants during the war. It seems as if politics were deep-rooted in the thinking of the majority of colonials at the time. In retrospect, it appears that the provincial congresses and committees of correspondence had a significant effect on Long Island, challenging the loyalties and political persuasions of inhabitants. These measures could be thought of as the beginnings of the warfare that pitted neighbor against neighbor.

Life and survival in general in the eighteenth century were hard. Living during a civil war and under the continued threat of a foreign military authority is unimaginable to us today. The hardships of many, it seems, continued after the war, and most likely, the legacy of the war remained in the minds of Long Islanders for more than a generation. Along with this remembrance was probably the need to forget the evils and violence of the war. Those sites that involved wartime violence were most likely cast off and destroyed rather quickly.

With this, the physical places that were the stages for stories and experiences of the British occupation of Long Island have mostly vanished. With this loss, we also lose the remembrance of what Long Islanders had to endure. This was truly their contribution to the war effort. Today, there is once again a responsibility to preserve and mark the places that remain so that future generations do not forget what the people of Long Island did to aid in the creation of this great American nation.

NOTES

Introduction

1. Force and Clarke. *American Archives*, 5th series, 1:1,121.
2. Ibid., 1:1,211–212.
3. Buck, "An Inspired Hoax," 202.
4. Gachot, "History of the Henry Post House," 10.
5. *Freeman's*, "Collectors' Story."
6. Naylor, "Surviving the Ordeal," 116.
7. Founders Online, "To George Washington from Major General Alexander McDougall, 11–15 January 1779," National Archives, https://founders. archives.gov/documents/Washington/03-18-02-0683 (original source: *The Papers of George Washington*, Revolutionary War Series, vol. 18, *1 November 1778–14 January 1779*, edited by Edward G. Lengel [Charlottesville: University of Virginia Press, 2008], 615–21).

Chapter 1: Quartering

8. Hedenburgh, "Memoranda of the Revolution in Newtown," 5.
9. McCurdy, *Quarters*, 13.
10. Onderdonk, *Jamaica Centennial*, 21.
11. McCurdy, *Quarters*, 16.
12. Hibbard, *Rock Hall*, 6.

13. *History of Queens County*, 38.
14. Onderdonk, *Documents and Letters*, 133.
15. Stoutenburgh, *Documentary History*, 787.
16. Earle, *Home Life*, 40.
17. Ibid.
18. Post, *Personal Recollections*, 34.
19. Ibid., 136.
20. *Freeman's*, "Collectors' Story."
21. Email from Ted Gachot (son of Richard Gachot), January 31, 2022.
22. Post, *Personal Recollections*, 136.
23. Seyfried, *Queens*, 27.
24. Wilson, *Historic Long Island*, 157–58.
25. Baldwin, "Local Revolutionary War Events," 90–91.
26. Long Island Genealogy, "List of Persons in Suffolk Co, Long Island, Who Took the Oath of Allegiance Before Governor Tryon."
27. MacMaster, *American Revolution in Queens*, 4.
28. Ibid., 5.
29. Founders Online, "To George Washington from Major General Alexander McDougall, 11–15 January 1779," https://founders.archives. gov/?q=Major%20General%20Alexander%20McDougall%20 Author%3A%22McDougall%2C%20Alexander%22&s=1511311111 &r=27.
30. Riker, *Annals of Newtown*, 210.
31. Peebles and Gruber, *Peebles' American War*, 231.
32. Bolton, *Relics of the Revolution*, 183.
33. Skillman, *Skillmans of New York*, 2.
34. Calver, "Discoveries Made," 133–34.
35. Meyer, *Irony of Submission*, 35.
36. Onderdonk, *Jamaica Centennial*, 23.

Chapter 2: Requisition

37. Darlington, "Long Island under Martial Law," 70.
38. Hagist and Atkinson, *Noble Volunteers*, 161.
39. Batten, "Long Island's Loyalists," 3–5.
40. Onderdonk, *Documents and Letters*, 191.
41. Founders Online, "To Washington from McDougall."
42. "Norton, Seth," Hartford, Connecticut Historical Society.

43. Simcoe, *Military Journal*, 93–94.
44. Darlington, "Long Island under Martial Law," 74.
45. Ibid., 71.
46. Ibid.
47. Onderdonk, Trow, Crombie, et al., *Revolutionary Incidents*, 86.
48. Ibid.
49. Tiedemann, "Patriots by Default," 44.
50. Staudt, "Wretchedness to Independence," 142.
51. Document containing Timothy Carll's claims against British forces, 1779. Revolutionary War claims, Huntington Town Clerk's Archives manuscript collection, https://nyheritage.contentdm.oclc.org/digital/collection/p16373 coll130/id/371/rec/1.
52. Street, *Huntington Town Records*, 13.
53. Blydenburgh Manuscripts, "Inhabitants of Smithtown v. King George III."
54. Blank, "Census of 1781," 3.
55. Ibid.,4–5.
56. WikiTree, "Jesse Platt Jr."
57. Platt, "Old Times in Huntington," 39.
58. Sammis, *Huntington-Babylon*, 234.
59. Long Island Surnames, "Platt Carll."
60. Reynolds, *Long Island Behind the British Lines*, 10.
61. Longwood Journey, "Committee of Safety at Coram."
62. Ibid.
63. "L.I. House Property," *County Review.*
64. White, *Tillotson Family*, 10.
65. "L.I. House Property," *County Review.*
66. Brooks, *History of the Fanning Family*, 140.
67. Pumpelly, "Historical Sketches," 230.
68. O'Sullivan, *East Hampton and the American Revolution*, 48.
69. Ibid., 48–49.
70. *Orderly book of the Maryland Loyalists Regiment*, 22–34.
71. Craven, *History of Mattituck*, 119.
72. Jefferson, *Southold and Its People*, 25.

Chapter 3: Plundering

73. Hagist and Atkinson, *Noble Volunteers*, 169.
74. Tiedemann, "Patriots by Default," 40.

75. Conway, "To Subdue America," 385.

76. Hedenburgh, "Memoranda of the Revolution in Newtown," 1.

77. Ibid, 7.

78. Platt, "Old Times in Huntington," 50–53.

79. Post, *Personal Recollections*, 40–41.

80. "Revolutionary Incidents #8," *Northport Journal*, 1A.

81. Bayles, "Tales of Middle Island."

82. Gass, *History of Miller's Place*, 22.

83. Hagist and Atkinson, *Noble Volunteers*, 173.

84. Strong, "Gone to Yorke," 173.

85. Hagist and Atkinson, *Noble Volunteers*, 159.

86. Ibid., 160.

87. *Junto*, "Edifying Terror," 1.

88. Ibid., 174.

Chapter 4: Abuses

89. Tiedemann, "Patriots by Default," 38.

90. Ibid.

91. Ibid., 39.

92. Ibid., 50.

93. Ibid., 42.

94. Staudt, "Wretchedness to Independence," 142.

95. Borthwick, *Church at the South*, 124–25.

96. Floyd, "Manuscript of Address."

97. Borthwick, *Church at the South*, 191.

98. Post, *Personal Recollections*, 27.

99. Ibid., 166.

100. Davis Town Meeting House Society, "Desk of Goldsmith Davis."

101. Onderdonk, Trow, Crombie, et al., *Revolutionary Incidents*, 102.

102. *History of Queens County*, 83.

103. "Picqueting," *New York Journal* 2, no. 118 (August 11, 1810): 2.

104. Naylor, "Surviving the Ordeal," 123.

105. Tiedemann, "Patriots by Default," 60.

106. Ibid.

107. Onderdonk, *Documents and Letters*, 198.

108. Loyalist Muster Rolls, National Archives of Canada RG 8, series I ("C" series), vol. 1,895.

109. Onderdonk, Trow, Crombie, et al., *Revolutionary Incidents*, 109.

110. Boombridge Genealogy, "Nathaniel Parker."

111. Lott, "Caumsette," 64.

112. Wiener, *Civilians Under Military Justice*, 278.

113. Onderdonk, *Documents and Letters*, 148.

114. Dandridge, "William Cunningham."

115. *Junto*, "Edifying Terror," 1.

116. Platt, "Old Times in Huntington," 65–66.

117. "Youthful Rebel," *Brooklyn Daily Eagle*.

Chapter 5: Dragoons

118. *Secondat*, "17th Light Dragoons."

119. Ibid.

120. Ibid.

121. Founders Online, "To Washington from Captain Lewis J. Costigin, 13 December 1778," https://founders.archives.gov/?q=Captain%20Lewis%20J.%20Costigin&s=1511311111&r=3.

122. Marshall and Oman, *Colonial Hempstead*, 319.

123. Hinde, *Discipline of the Light-Horse*, 99–100.

124. Post, *Personal Recollections*, 162.

125. Strong, "Dreaded Colonel Birch," 69.

126. Ibid.

127. Marshall and Oman, *Colonial Hempstead*, 320.

128. "Boys Unearth Skeleton," *New York Times*.

129. Tarlow and Lowman, *Harnessing the Power*, 153.

130. Ibid., 154.

131. "Skeleton Is Held," *New York Times*.

132. Onderdonk, *Documents and Letters*, 148.

133. Muster Books and Pay Lists (WO 12/1306): 17th Light Dragoons: 1772–1783, Microfilm Record, Harriet Irving Library, Loyalist Collection, University of New Brunswick, Charlottetown, NB.

134. Tarlow and Lowman, *Harnessing the Power*, 160.

135. Van Santvoord, "Simcoe's Fort," 9.

136. Simcoe, *Military Journal*, 97.

137. Ibid, 98.

138. Sherman, "Captain Diemar's Regiment," 5.

139. Corrado and Zebrowski, *Black Hussars*, 7–8.

140. Van Santvoord, "Simcoe's Fort," 9.
141. "State of Particular Companies of the Provincial Corps for a General Muster &ca Feby. 1779," Dreer Collection, misc. mss no. 11, Historical Society of Pennsylvania.
142. Seth Norton, Revolutionary War papers, Hofstra University's Long Island Studies Institute, Nassau County Museum Reference Collection, 1775.
143. General Court Martial of Thomas Connoly, n.p.
144. Ibid.
145. Loyalist Muster Rolls, National Archives of Canada RG 8, series I ("C" series), vol. 1, 895.
146. Royal Provincial, "King's American Dragoons Proposal."

Chapter 6: Hessians

147. Hall, "French and Hessian Impressions," 4.
148. Londahl-Smidt and Trexler, German Troops, 4–5.
149. Wallace, "Hessians on Long Island," 1A.
150. Ibid.
151. Ibid.
152. Onderdonk, *Documents and Letters*, 151.
153. Hall, "French and Hessian Impressions," 9.
154. Kemble, *Journals of Lieut. Col. Stephen Kemble*, 91.
155. Onderdonk, *Documents and Letters*, 249.
156. Hedenburgh, "Memoranda of the Revolution in Newtown," 5.
157. Hall, "French and Hessian Impressions," 9.
158. Von Kraft, *Journal*, 82.
159. Von Ewald and Tustin, *Diary of the American War*, 250.
160. Ibid., 251.
161. Onderdonk, *Queens County in Olden Times*, 64.
162. Post, *Personal Recollections*, 76.
163. Great Britain, *Report on American Manuscripts*, 457.
164. Schenawolf, "Hessian Soldier's Letter Home," N.p.
165. "Letters from Private Jung Heim Steller," *Journal of the Johannes Schwalm Historical Association*, 1.
166. Wust, "Military Immigration," 40.
167. Onderdonk, *Documents and Letters*, 243.
168. "Lt. Col v. Wurmb, 9 April 81," Freiherr von Jungkenn Papers, William L. Clements Library, University of Michigan.

Chapter 7: Raiders

169. Overton, *Plunderers from Across the Sound*, 3.

170. Ibid.

171. Post, *Personal Recollections*, 75.

172. Ibid., 106.

173. Mather, *Refugees of 1776*, 204.

174. Post, *Personal Recollections*, 105–6.

175. Gass, *History of Miller's Place*, 22.

176. Ibid., 20.

177. Jefferson, *Southold and Its People*, 34.

178. Onderdonk, Trow, Crombie, et al., *Revolutionary Incidents*, 73.

179. Post, *Personal Recollections*, 128–29.

180. Tiedemann, *Thomas Jones*, n.p.

181. Ibid.

182. Mather, *Refugees of 1776*, 1,056.

183. Founders Online, "To George Washington from William Duer, 2 March 1777," National Archives (Original source: *The Papers of George Washington*, Revolutionary War Series, vol. 18, *1 November 1778–14 January 1779*, edited by Edward G. Lengel [Charlottesville: University of Virginia Press, 2008], 478–86).

184. "Suffolk County New York Militia to Clinton, Mar. 10, 1778," University of Michigan, William L. Clements Library, Sir Henry Clinton Papers, vol. 32, item 1.

185. Onderdonk, Trow, Crombie, et al., *Revolutionary Incidents*, 86.

186. Onderdonk, *Documents and Letters*, 184.

187. Post, *Personal Recollections*, 156.

188. Onderdonk, *Documents and Letters*, 185.

189. "Abstracts of Wills on File in the Surrogate's Office, City of New York, 1665–1801," vol. 10, October 28, 1780–November 5, 1782, Collections of the New York Historical Society for the Year 1901, Publication Fund Series, New York: Printed for the Society.

190. Grumman, *Revolutionary Soldiers of Redding*, 16.

191. Onderdonk, *Documents and Letters*, 185.

Chapter 8: Quakers

192. Brock, *Pioneers*, 141.

193. Post, *Personal Recollections*, 114–15.
194. Crotty, "Times of Peril," 52.
195. Brock, *Pioneers*, 180.
196. Crotty, "Times of Peril," 56.
197. Gachot, "History of the Henry Post House," 5.
198. Crotty, "Times of Peril," 58.
199. Gachot, "History of the Henry Post House," 6.
200. Barbour, *Quaker Crosscurrents*, 53.
201. Brock, *Pioneers*, 182.
202. Post, *Personal Recollections*, 55.
203. Onderdonk, *Queens County in Olden Times*, 60.
204. Wilbur, *Life and Labors of Elias Hicks*, 16–17.
205. Hicks, Hicks and Seaman, *Life and Religious Labours of E. Hicks*, 20.
206. Tiedemann, "Queens County, New York Quakers," 224.
207. Brock, *Pioneers*, 181.
208. Tiedemann, "Queens County, New York Quakers," 224.

Chapter 9: Refugees

209. Mather, *Refugees of 1776*, 166.
210. Ibid., 167.
211. Fish, *New York State*, 249.
212. Borthwick, *Church at the South*, 122.
213. Mather, *Refugees of 1776*, 170.
214. Col. Josiah Smith Papers.
215. Mather, *Refugees of 1776*, 171.
216. Borthwick, *Church at the South*, 123.
217. Ibid., 124.
218. Ibid.
219. Wallace, "Northport's Revolutionary Refugees," 1A.
220. Meyer, *Irony of Submission*, 19.
221. Onderdonk, *Queens County in Olden Times*, 57.
222. Meyer, *Irony of Submission*, 21.
223. Davidson, *Burdens of Loyalty*, 204–5.
224. Ibid., 199.
225. Onderdonk, Trow, Crombie, et al., *Revolutionary Incidents*, 230.
226. Founders Online, "To George Washington from William Stephens Smith, 1 September 1783," https://founders.archives.gov/?q=%20

Author%3A%22Smith%2C%20William%20Stephens%22%201%20 september%201783&s=1511311111&r=2&sr=.

227. Founders Online, "To George Washington from William Stephens Smith, 3 October 1783," https://founders.archives.gov/documents/Washington /99-01-02-11896.

228. Batten, "Long Island's Loyalists," 3–5, 19.

229. Ibid., 5.

Epilogue

230. Batten, "Long Island's Loyalists," 5.

231. Wilson, *Historic Long Island*, 162.

BIBLIOGRAPHY

Primary Sources

"Abstracts of Wills on File in the Surrogate's Office, City of New York, 1665–1801." Vol. 10. October 28, 1780–November 5, 1782. Collections of the New York Historical Society for the Year 1901. Publication Fund Series. New York: Printed for the Society.

Blydenburgh Manuscripts. "Inhabitants of Smithtown v. King George III." 1783. Transcribed from the original document. Smithtown Historical Society, Smithtown, NY.

Col. Josiah Smith Papers. J. Conklin Havens estate. Suffolk County Historical Society Archives, Riverhead, NY.

Crackel, Theodore J., ed. *Papers of George Washington*. Charlotesville: University of Virginia Press, Rotunda, 2008. Digital edition.

Document containing Timothy Carll's claims against British forces, 1779. Revolutionary War claims. Huntington Town Clerk's Archives manuscript collection. https://nyheritage.contentdm.oclc.org/digital/collection/p16373coll130/id/371/rec/1.

Force, Peter, and M. St. Clair Clarke. *American Archives: Consisting of a Collection of Authentick Records State Papers Debates and Letters and Other Notices of Publick Affairs the Whole Forming a Documentary History of the Origin and Progress of the North American Colonies; of the Causes and Accomplishment of the American Revolution; and of the Constitution of Government for the United States to the Final Ratification Thereof.* Washington, D.C.: Published by M. St. Clair Clarke and Peter Force, 1837.

Founders Online. "Crackel, Theodore J., ed. *The Papers of George Washington.* Charlotesville: University of Virginia Press, Rotunda, 2008. Digital Edition." https://founders.archives.gov/?q=Project%3A%22Washington%20 Papers%22&s=1511211111&r=1.

General Court Martial of Thomas Connoly, 1779. Great Britain, Public Record Office, War Office, class 71, volume 88, 341–44.

Great Britain. *Report on American Manuscripts in the Royal Institution of Great Britain.* Vol. 4. London: HMSO, 1904–9. http://catalog.hathitrust.org/ api/volumes/oclc/530556129.html.

Hedenburgh, James. "Memoranda of the Revolution in Newtown as Recorded by Rev. John Goldsmith from Persons Still Surviving." Newtown, Queens County, NY. 1846.

Hicks, Elias, Valentine Hicks and Robert Seaman. *Journal of the Life and Religious Labours of E. Hicks. Written by Himself.* 3rd ed. Edited by V. Hicks and R. Seaman. London: British Library, 1832. http://books.google. co.uk/books?vid=BL:A0019237012.

Hinde, Robert. *The Discipline of the Light-Horse: By Captain Hinde of the Royal Regiment of Foresters (Light-Dragoons.) Illustrated with Copper Plates.* London: Printed for W. Owen in Fleet Street, 1778. http://books.google.com/ books?id=jB5EAAAAYAAJ.

Howell, George Rogers. *The Early History of Southampton, L.I., New York with Genealogies.* Albany, NY: Weed, Parsons and Company, 1887.

John Graves Simcoe Papers, 1774–1824. Correspondence and documents, William L. Clements Library, University of Michigan.

Jones, Thomas, and Edward F. De Lancey. History of New York During the Revolutionary War. New York: Printed for the New York Historical Society. 1879.

Kemble, Stephen. *Journals of Lieut. Col. Stephen Kemble, 1773–1789: And British Army Orders: Gen. Sir William Howe, 1775–1778; Gen. Sir Henry Clinton, 1778; and Gen. Daniel Jones, 1778.* New York: Ardent Media, 1972.

"Letters from Private Jung Heim Steller to His Parents, 1777–1778." Translated by Henry Retzer. Annotated by Donald Londahl-Smidt. *Journal of the Johannes Schwalm Historical Association* 5, no. 2 (1994): 1.

Long Island Genealogy. "A List of Persons in Suffolk Co, Long Island, Who Took the Oath of Allegiance Before Governor Tryon, 24 November 1778." http://longislandgenealogy.com/1778_Census_&_Oath_Southold%20 NY.pdf.

Loyalist Muster Rolls. National Archives of Canada RG 8, series I ("C" series), vol. 1, 895.

"Lt. Col v. Wurmb, 9 April 81." Freiherr von Jungkenn Papers, William L. Clements Library, University of Michigan.

Muster Books and Pay Lists (WO 12/1306): 17th Light Dragoons: 1772–1783. Microfilm Record, Harriet Irving Library, University of New Brunswick, Charlottetown, NB.

Norton, Seth. Revolutionary War Papers, Hofstra University's Long Island Studies Institute, Nassau County Museum Reference Collection, 1775.

"Norton, Seth. 1777–1781. Seth Norton Incoming Correspondence." Hartford, Connecticut Historical Society.

Onderdonk, Henry. *Jamaica Centennial, July 4th, 1876.* Jamaica: L.I.: n.p., 1876.

———. *Queens County in Olden Times: Being a Supplement to the Several Histories Thereof.* Jamaica, NY: C. Welling, 1865. http://www.accessible.com/accessible/preLog?Browse=BNY001308.

Onderdonk, H., J.F. Trow and J.N. Crombie et al. *Revolutionary Incidents of Suffolk and Kings Counties: With an Account of the Battle of Long Island and the British Prisons and Prison-Ships at New York.* New York: Leavitt & Company, 1849.

Onderdonk, Henry, Jr. *Documents and Letters Intended to Illustrate the Revolutionary Incidents of Queens County: With Connecting Narratives, Explanatory Notes, and Additions.* New York: Leavitt, Trow and Company, 1846.

———. *Documents and Letters Intended to Illustrate the Revolutionary Incidents of Queens County: With Connecting Narratives, Explanatory Notes, and Additions.* Second series. Hempstead: Lott Van de Water, 1884.

Orderly Book of the Maryland Loyalists Regiment, June 18th, 1778, to October 12th, 1778. Kept by Captain Caleb Jones. Edited by Paul L. Ford. Brooklyn, NY: Historical Printing Club, 1891.

Orderly Book of the Three Battalions of Loyalist Commanded by Brigadier-General Oliver De Lancey 1776–1778. Baltimore, MD: Geneological Publishing Co, 1972.

Peebles, John, and Ira D. Gruber. *John Peebles' American War: The Diary of a Scottish Grenadier, 1776–1782.* Stroud, Gloucestershire, UK: Published by Sutton for the Army Records Society, 1997.

"Picqueting." *New York Journal* 2, no. 118 (August 11, 1810): 2.

Platt, Henry C. "Old Times in Huntington." Historical address delivered at the centennial celebration in Huntington, Suffolk County, NY, July 1876.

Post, Lydia Minturn. *Personal Recollections of the American Revolution. A Private Journal. Prepared from Authentic Domestic Records. Together with Reminiscences of Washington & Lafayette.* Edited by Sidney Barclay (pseud.). New York: Rudd & Carleton, 1859.

"Rep. No.: L55.16.1, Original List. List of British Soldiers Quartered at Jericho, 1783." Long Island Studies Institute Collections, Nassau County Museum, Hempstead, NY.

Riker, James, Jr. *The Annals of Newtown in Queens County, New York.* New York: D. Fanshaw, 1852.

Robertson, Archibald. *Archibald Robertson Lieutenant-General Royal Engineers, His Diaries and Sketches in America 1762–1780.* Edited by Harry Miller Lydenberg. New York: New York Public Library, 1930.

Ross, Peter, and William S. Pelletreau. *History of Long Island, From Its Earliest Settlement to the Present Time.* Vol. 2. New York: Lewis Publishing Company, 1905.

Royal Provincial. "King's American Dragoons Proposal, Great Britain, Public Record Office, Headquarters Papers of the British Army in America, PRO 30/55/2812." https://www.royalprovincial.com/military/musters/kad/kadupham1.htm, June 4, 2020.

Simcoe, John Graves (lieutenant colonel). *Simcoe's Military Journal. A History of the Operations of a Partisan Corps called the Queen's Rangers, Commanded by Lieut. Col. J.G. Simcoe, During the War of the American Revolution.* New York: Bartlett & Welford, 1844.

"State of Particular Companies of the Provincial Corps for a General Muster &ca Feby. 1779." Dreer Collection, misc. mss no. 11, Historical Society of Pennsylvania.

Street, Charles R. *Huntington Town Records, Including Babylon, Long Island, New York (1776–1873).* Vol. 3. Huntington, NY: n.p., 1887.

"Suffolk County New York Militia to Clinton, Mar. 10, 1778." University of Michigan, William L. Clements Library, Sir Henry Clinton Papers, vol. 32, item 1.

University of Michigan Library Digital Collections. "A Map of the Pass at Jamaica, Long Island: Surveyed by Order of His Excellency General Sir Henry Clinton K.B. Commander in Chief of His Majesty's Forces & Co. March 1782/by George Taylor, Capt. of Guides." https://quod.lib.umich.edu/w/wcl1ic/x-8673/wcl008744.

———. "Part of the Southwestern Shore of Long Island." https://quod.lib.umich.edu/w/wcl1ic/x-848/wcl000942.

Von Ewald, Johann, and Joseph Philips Tustin. *Diary of the American War: A Hessian Journal.* New Haven, CT: Yale University Press, 1979.

Von Kraft, John Charles Philip. *Journal of Lieutenant John Charles Philip von Kraft.* New York: New York Times, 1968.

Secondary Sources

Allen, Thomas B., and Todd W. Braisted. *The Loyalist Corps: Americans in Service to the King.* Takoma Park, MD: Foxacre Press, 2011.

Baldwin, Richard P. "Local Revolutionary War Events." *Suffolk County Historical Society Register* 27, no. 3. (1999): 90–91.

Barbour, Hugh. *Quaker Crosscurrents: Three Hundred Years of Friends in the New York Yearly Meetings.* 1st ed. Syracuse, NY: Syracuse University Press, 1995.

Batten, Andrew C. "Long Island's Loyalists: The Misunderstood Americans." *Freeholder* 3, no. 4, (Spring 1999): 3–5.

Bayles, Thomas R. "Tales of Middle Island." *Patchogue Advance*, July 21, 1949.

Blank, John A. "The Census of 1781. (Part 1)." *Nassau County Historical Society* 13, no. 1 (October 1951): 1–9.

Bolton, Reginald Pelham. *Relics of the Revolution: The Story of the Discovery of the Buried Remains of Military Life in Forts and Camps on Manhattan Island.* New York: self-published, 1916.

Boombridge Genealogy. "Nathaniel Parker, 1740s–1783." https://boombridgegenealogy.com/getperson.php?personID=I63837&tree=4February2018.

Borthwick, George. *The Church at the South: A History of the South Haven Church.* Cutchogue, NY: George Borthwick Cutchogue Presbyterian Church, 1989.

Brock, Peter. *Pioneers of the Peaceable Kingdom.* Princeton, NJ: Princeton University Press, 1968 and 1970.

Brooklyn Daily Eagle. "Youthful Rebel Who Lived Here Plagued British Soldiers Who Annoyed Huntington Residents." February 7, 1924. http://www.brooklynpubliclibrary.org/eagle/.

Brooks, Walter Frederic. *History of the Fanning Family: A Genealogical Record to 1900 of the Descendants of Edmund Fanning the Emigrant Ancestor in America Who Settled in Connecticut in 1653; to Which Is Prefixed a General Account of the Fanning Family in Europe from Norman Times 1197 to the Cromwellian Confiscations 1652–3.* Salem, MA: Higginson Book, n.d. http://catalog.hathitrust.org/api/volumes/oclc/28385191.html.

Buck, Sarah. "An Inspired Hoax: The Antebellum Reconstruction of an Eighteenth-Century Long Island Diary." *Long Island Historical Journal* 7, no. 2 (1995): 191–204.

Calver, William L. "Discoveries Made in British Camps of the American Revolution." *Quarterly Journal of the New York State Historical Association* 8, no. 2 (1927): 133–42. http://www.jstor.org/stable/43565058.

Calver, William Louis, and Reginald Pelham Bolton. *History Written with Pick and Shovel: Military Buttons Belt-Plates Badges and Other Relics Excavated from Colonial Revolutionary and War of 1812 Camp Sites by the Field Exploration Committee of the New York Historical Society.* New York: New York Historical Society, 1950.

Conway, Stephen. "To Subdue America: British Army Officers and the Conduct of the Revolutionary War." *William and Mary Quarterly* 43, no. 3 (1986): 381–407. https://doi.org/10.2307/1922482.

Cooper, Laura. "A Brief History of the Canoe Place Inn." *Southampton Press*, November 23, 2010.

Corrado, Gary, and Stephanie Zebrowski. *The Black Hussars: A Brief and Concise History of Frederick Diemar's Hussars.* Westminister, MD: Heritage Books. 2005.

County Review. "L.I. House Property Has Long History." March 28, 1924.

Craven, Charles E. *A History of Mattituck Long Island N.Y.* Mattituck, NY: J. Clauss & Sons, 1988.

Crotty, Joseph John. "'Times of Peril': Quakers in British-Occupied New York During the American Revolution, 1775–1783." *Quaker History* 106, no. 2 (2017): 45–71. http://www.jstor.org/stable/45180030.

Dandridge, Dansk. "William Cunningham, Monster." *American Primer.* https://www.theamericanprimer.com/index.php/categories/american-revolution-2/120-william-cunningham-murderer.

Darlington, Oscar G. "Long Island under Martial Law." *Nassau County Historical Journal* 5, no. 2 (Fall 1942): 70–79.

Davidson, Stephen E. *The Burdens of Loyalty: Refugee Tales from the First American Civil War.* Saint John: United Empire Loyalists' Association of Canada, New Brunswick, 2015.

Davis Town Meeting House Society. "The Desk of Goldsmith Davis, An Oral History of the Desk as Told to Harriett and Jeanette Bedell, Great-Great-Granddaughters of Goldsmith Davis." September 5, 1933. http://www.davistownmeetinghouse.org/resources/Goldsmith+Davis-Desk.pdf.

Earle, A.M. *Home Life in Colonial Days.* Mineola, NY: Dover Pub, 1975.

Email from Ted Gachot (the son of Richard Gachot). January 31, 2022.

Fish, Hamilton. *New York State: The Battleground of the Revolutionary War.* 1st ed. New York: Vantage Press, 1976.

Floyd, Augustus. "Manuscript of Address of Suffolk County in Revolutionary Days Before the Suffolk County Historical Society, Feb. 24, 1897." From the Archives of the Suffolk County Historical Society, Riverhead, NY.

Freeman's. "The Collectors' Story: Richard & Irene Gachot." 2019. https://www.freemansauction.com/news/collectors-story-richard-irene-gachot/.

Gachot, Richard. "A History of the Henry Post House, Built 1762." Westbury, NY.

Gass, Margaret Davis. *History of Miller's Place.* Rev. ed. New York: St. Gerard Printing, 1987.

Grumman, William Edgar. *The Revolutionary Soldiers of Redding Connecticut and the Record of Their Services.* Hartford, CT: Hartford Press, the Case Lockwood & Brainard Company, 1904. https://archive.org/details/revolutionarysol00grum.

Hagist, Don N., and Rick Atkinson. *Noble Volunteers: The British Soldiers Who Fought the American Revolution.* Yardley, PA: Westholme Publishing LLC, 2020.

Hall, Cosby Williams. "French and Hessian Impressions: Foreign Soldiers' Views of America during the Revolution." PhD diss., College of William and Mary, 2003.

Halsey, William Donaldson. *Sketches from Local History.* Bridgehampton, NY: H. Lee, 1935.

Hibbard, Shirley G. *Rock Hall: A Narrative History.* Hempstead, NY: Friends of the Rock Hall Inc., in association with Dover Publications, 1997.

History of Queens County with Illustrations, Portraits & Sketches of Prominent Families and Individuals. New York: W.W. Munsell & Co., 1882.

Jefferson, Wayland. *Southold and Its People in the Revolutionary Days.* Southold, NY: L.I. Traveler Print, 1932.

Junto: A Group Blog on Early American History. "Edifying Terror: Publicity and the Problem of Punishment." October 2, 2015. https://earlyamericanists.com/2015/10/02/edifying-terror-publicity-and-the-problem-of-punishment/.

Londahl-Smidt, Donald M., and Jeff Trexler. German Troops in the American Revolution. Vol. 1. Hessen-Cassel. Oxford, UK: Osprey Publishing, 2021.

Long Island Surnames. "Platt Carll (1734–1814)." http://longislandsurnames.com/getperson.php?personID=I04286&tree=Platt.

Longwood Journey. "Record of Hay, Purchased and Stored at Coram." Bill and transcription provided by Margaret Davis Gass. https://sites.google.com/longwoodcsd.org/longwoodjourney/time-periods/american-revolution/the-burning-of-the-hay-at-coram/bill-for-hay-purchased-by-the-british.

Lott, Roy E. "Caumsette: A Gift of Love." *Long Island Forum* 29, no. 4 (April 1966): 63–64.

Luke, Myron H., and Robert W. Venables. *Long Island in the American Revolution.* Albany: New York State American Revolution Bicentennial Commission, 1976.

MacMaster, Frank J. *The American Revolution in Queens: Revolutionary War Sites in Flushing and Jamaica Bayside Douglaston Hollis and Whitestone in the Borough of Queens.* Queens, NY: Borough Historian, 1961.

Marshall, Bernice Schultz, and Mary Irish Oman. *Colonial Hempstead: Long Island Life Under the Dutch and English.* 2nd ed. Port Washington, NY: I.J. Friedman, 1962.

Mather, Frederic Gregory. *The Refugees of 1776 from Long Island to Connecticut.* Albany, NY: J.B. Lyon Company Printers, 1913.

McCurdy, J.G. *Quarters: The Accommodation of the British Army and the Coming of the American Revolution.* Ithica, NY: Cornell University Press, 2019.

Meyer, Lois J. *The Irony of Submission: The British Occupation of Huntington and Long Island, 1776–1783.* N.p.: R.B. Langhans, 1992.

Naylor, Natalie A. "Surviving the Ordeal: Long Island Women During the Revolutionary War." *Long Island Historical Journal* 20, nos. 1–2 (Fall 2007/Spring 2008): 114–34.

New York Times. "Boys Unearth Skeleton in Torture Cage; Discovery in Hempstead Linked to Pirates." December 29, 1934. https://www.nytimes.com/1934/12/29/archives/boys-unearth-skeleton-in-torture-cage-discovery-in-hempstead-linked.html.

———. "Skeleton Is Held That of an Indian." December 30, 1934. https://www.nytimes.com/1934/12/30/archives/skeleton-is-held-that-of-an-indian-bones-dug-up-in-hempstead-those.html.

O'Sullivan, Ilse. *East Hampton and the American Revolution.* Edited by Frances Colley and Norman Reader. East Hampton, NY: Publication of the East Hampton Town Bicentennial Committee, 1976.

Overton, Albert G. *Plunderers from Across the Sound: Documented Narratives of Revoultionary [sic] War Incidents Not Previously Known to Historians Involving Inhabitants of Long Island Connecticut and Nantucket in the Illicit Trade and Raids Across the Sound.* Florissant, MO: Micro-Records Pub., 1980.

Post, Marie Caroline. *The Post Family.* New York: Sterling Potter, 1905.

Pumpelly, Josiah C. "Historical Sketches of the Hampton Settlements on Long Island." *Americana* 6 (January 1911–December 1911): 230.

"Revolutionary Incidents #8 Hung by the British." *Northport Journal* 124, no. 9 (September 3, 1998): 1A.

Reynolds, John. *Long Island Behind the British Lines During the Revolution.* Setauket, NY: Society for the Preservation of Long Island Antiquities, 1960.

Sammis, Romanah. *Huntington-Babylon Town History.* Huntington, NY: Huntington Historical Society, 1937.

Schenawolf, Harry "A Hessian Soldier's Letter Home Describes Colonial America, Describing Staten and Long Island 1776." *Revolutionary War Journal* (September 19, 2013). https://www.revolutionarywarjournal. com/hessian-soldiers-letter-home/.

Secondat. "The 17th Light Dragoons in Newtown Queens." September 24, 2011. http://secondat.blogspot.com/2011/09/17th-light-dragoons-in-newtown-queens.html.

Seyfried, Vincent F. *Queens: A Pictorial History.* Norfolk, VA: Donning, 1982.

Sherman, Constance D. "Captain Diemar's Regiment of Hussars on Long Island." *Journal of Long Island History* 5, no. 3 (Summer 1965): 1–16.

Skillman, Francis. *The Skillmans of New York.* Compiled by Francis Skillman of Roslyn. NY: Jones & Co., 1892.

Staudt, John G. "From Wretchedness to Independence: Suffolk County in the American Revolution." *Long Island Historical Journal* 20, nos. 1–2 (2007–8):135–62.

Stoutenburgh, H.A. *A Documentary History of Het (the) Nederdeutsche Gemeente Dutch Congregation of Oyster Bay Queens County Island of Nassau Now Long Island.* New York: Knickerbocker Press, 1902–7.

Strong, Kate W. "The Dreaded Colonel Birch." *Long Island Forum* 13, no. 4 (April 1950): 69.

———. "Gone to Yorke." *Long Island Forum* 3, no. 8 (August 1940): 173.

———. "When Smithtown Was Plundered." *Long Island Forum* 14, no. 1 (January 1951): 7–8.

Tarlow, Sarah, and Emma Battell Lowman. *Harnessing the Power of the Criminal Corpse.* 1st ed. Cham, DE: Springer International Publishing, an imprint of Palgrave Macmillan, 2018. https://doi.org/10.1007/978-3-319-77908-9.

Tiedemann, Joseph S. "Patriots by Default: Queens County, New York, and the British Army, 1776–1783." *William and Mary Quarterly* 43, no. 1 (1986): 35–63. https://doi.org/10.2307/1919356.

———. "Queens County, New York Quakers in the American Revolution: Loyalists or Neutrals?" *Historical Magazine of the Protestant Episcopal Church* 52, no. 3 (1983): 215–27. http://www.jstor.org/stable/42973965.

———. *Thomas Jones: Embittered Long Island Loyalist.* Stony Brook, NY: Center for Global & Local History, a unit of the Stony Brook Institute for Global Studies, 2009. https://lihj.cc.stonybrook.edu/2009/articles/thomas-jones-embittered-long-island-loyalist/.

Todd W. Braisted. The On-Line Institute for Advanced Loyalist Studies. February 7, 2015. http://www.royalprovincial.com/index.html.

Van Santvoord, Peter L. "Colonel Simcoe's Fort." Long Island Forum 27, no. 1 (1964): 9–12.

Wallace, George. "The Hessians on Long Island." *Long Islander's Northport Journal* 133, no. 45 (December 6, 2007): 1A.

———. "Northport's Revolutionary Refugees." *Long Islander's Northport Journal* 129, no. 50 (September 25, 2003): 1A.

White, Willis H. *The Tillotson Family of Long Island New York: Three Generations of the Descendants of Samuel Tillotson.* Herndon, VA: W.H. White, 2001.

Wiener, Frederick Bernays. *Civilians Under Military Justice.* Chicago, IL: Universiy of Chicago Press, 1967. https://archives.albany.edu/concern/daos/cf95js48k?locale=en#?c=0&m=0&s=0&cv=0&xywh=574%2C2006%2C2706%2C1476

WikiTree. "Jesse Platt Jr. (1728–1769)." https://www.wikitree.com/wiki/Platt-2092.

Wilbur, Henry Watson. *The Life and Labors of Elias Hicks.* Philadelphia, PA: Friends' General Conference Advancement Committee, 1910. https://search.ebscohost.com/login.aspx?direct=true&db=h8h&bquery=(HJ5V2L)&type=1&site=ehost-live.

Wilson, Rufus Rockwell. *Historic Long Island.* New York: Berkeley Press, 1902. http://books.google.com/books?id=eCMVAAAAYAAJ.

Wines, Virginia, and the Suffolk County Historical Society. *Pioneers of Riverhead Town.* Riverhead, NY: Suffolk County Historical Society, 1981.

Wust, Klaus G. "Military Immigration from German Lands 1776–1783." *Society for the History of the Germans in Maryland* 44 (2000): 33–48.

ABOUT THE AUTHOR

David M. Griffin is an independent researcher and author whose interest has been in studying colonial era–built works and histories of the Revolutionary War period in the New York City region.

He is author of *Lost British Forts of Long Island* (The History Press, 2017) and coauthor with the Lamar Institute of *The Struggle for Long Island: Expanding Revolutionary War Studies in New York* (2019), an extensive report that records and analyzes three fortification battlefield sites on the north shore of Long Island. He is an active contributor and author for the online *Journal of the American Revolution*.

He holds a professional degree in architecture from Carleton University in Ottawa, Canada, and presently consults and practices in the fields of architecture and interior design within the New York area. He lives on the north shore of Long Island.